IN
HOLY FEAR

Rediscovering
the Fear of the Lord

by

Alistair Petrie

BOOKS BY THE SAME AUTHOR

GOD'S DESIGN FOR CHALLENGING TIMES
Discovering Freedom in an Age of Compromise

CHI–Books, Brisbane, 2014

> Available worldwide from online suppliers including:
> www.amazon.com | www.koorong.com | www.bookdepository.co.uk | www.wesleyowen.com
> eBook available from:
> Amazon Kindle | Apple iBookstore | Barnes & Noble | Wesley Owen | Chapters | Koorong.com

TRANSFORMED! PEOPLES – CITIES – NATIONS
10 Principles for Sustaining Genuine Revival

Chosen Books, Grand Rapids, MI, 2003: Republished 2008, Sovereign World Ltd.

RELEASING HEAVEN ON EARTH

Chosen Books, Grand Rapids, MI, 2000: Republished 2008, Sovereign World Ltd.

IN
HOLY FEAR

Rediscovering
the Fear of the Lord

by

Alistair Petrie

**CHI
BOOKS**

WHAT OTHERS ARE SAYING ABOUT THIS BOOK...

Few things are as important in life as knowing the right foundations upon which to build, whether that is a nation, a business, a family, or even one's personal life. No one would think of building anything without understanding the proper foundation, and yet the Western Church has for years ignored one of the most critical foundational truths: *the fear of the Lord*. If the Scriptures tell us that "the fear of the Lord is the beginning of wisdom", then understanding what this is must be central to everything else. Books on the subject are amazingly rare, but Dr. Alistair Petrie has written one of the best. In *In Holy Fear — Rediscovering the Fear of the Lord,* he convincingly argues that the fear of the Lord is the missing key to sustained revival, the missing ingredient to intimacy with God, the missing prayer when it comes to impacting our cities with the Gospel. Many Christians don't want to focus on this, because they feel it runs contrary to grace. *Nothing could be further from the truth!*

This book clearly reveals the connection between walking in the fear of the Lord and developing satisfying intimacy with God. Petrie sounds an important alarm bell for the Church in this hour. In our effort to be relevant, we are in danger of shrinking God to fit our comfort zones, and thus risk calling people to a Gospel that isn't Biblical.

I urge every spiritual leader — pastors and mission leaders — to get cases of these books! In Holy Fear needs to be an indispensable part of any discipleship course.

Rev. Steve Fry
Senior Pastor — The Gate Community Church, Franklin, Tennessee, USA
President, Messenger Fellowship

Alistair Petrie, in the book *In Holy Fear — Rediscovering the Fear of the Lord, uniquely* and skilfully guides us into understanding of what a truly vibrant and empowering relationship with the Lord is. The many stories and analogies clearly help paint a visual of the importance of understanding the fear of the Lord. I resonated with the clarion wakeup call from any complacency so that we may have discernment for the days in which we are now living. I was reminded of God's warning in Zephaniah chapter 1, verse 12: "At that time I will search Jerusalem with lamps and punish those who are complacent..." Like Zephaniah, Alistair helps us to recognize that the Holy Spirit is going through the Church with lamps and shedding light on the dangers of complacency. Zephaniah had a huge influence in the Revivals and Reforms in the days of King Josiah. Today, we are in great need of Awakening in the Church if we are to see Transforming Revival and Reforms.

The message in this book is one critically needed today. Personally, I found the book quite engaging, encouraging and empowering.

In Holy Fear is not a challenge to measure up to some sort of man–made standards. Rather, by the Grace of God we can be fully awakened and aware of the times in which we live, and equipped to make a Kingdom difference in the lives of multitudes.

Doug Stringer
Founder–president, Somebody Cares America, Houston, Texas, USA
Somebody Cares International

This book must be read carefully and completely. The author is himself motivated by reverence and respect in how he handles truth. He clearly desires results in the lives of sincere Christians and motivated congregations and groups. If you have questions — READ ON, since Alistair is committed to CONTEXTUAL truth. He uses the Word of God with honor and respect but also expresses in his writing obvious concern for every reader.

This book is spiritual dynamite, meant to revolutionize as well as INFLUENCE the reader, not simply to instruct and edify. I wish every sincere Christian would come to this as an altar of Word AND Spirit.

Rick C. Howard
Pastor, Author, International Teacher — Rick C. Howard Ministries

I strongly recommend this book, because of the seriousness and urgency of the days in which we live. The fear of the Lord needs to take fresh priority in our teaching and ministry. Alistair's insights into moving in the power of the opposite spirit, and positioning our hearts to receive from God, and aligning our thoughts to God's thoughts, are like a personal wake up call.

This book is for every believer who is willing to receive teaching and instruction into how critical it is to know and to apply these deep truths of releasing the fear of the Lord fully in our lives.

Jill Southern–Jones
Centre Director, Ellel Ministries Pierrepont UK;
Regional Director of S E Asia and China

I urge you to read this book now! The compelling insights Alistair Petrie shares are for the whole Body of Christ. He not only unveils the transformational impact of fearing God, but also how you can understand and begin to personally walk in the Fear of the Lord. Your spiritual walk will move to a whole new level as you digest divine revelation.

Dr. Naomi Dowdy
President, Naomi Dowdy Ministries — Founder, Chancellor, TCA College

The Bible has plenty to say about the fear of the Lord and it's vital that we take heed of these truths in this critical hour where many are compromising God's Word.

In this timely book, Alistair Petrie opens our eyes to the benefits of operating in the fear of the Lord, how the fear of man will hold you back from your destiny, how to pray in the opposite spirit to that of your persecutors and so much more. Seasoned Christians and new believers alike need to grab hold of the revelation in this book!

Jennifer LeClaire
Senior Editor, Charisma magazine USA; Author,
Director, Awakening House of Prayer

In his own inimitable way, Alistair excels in encouraging, informing and challenging us on a subject that is essential reading to every Christian in the Global Church.

Through Scripture, storytelling and his personal journey, he removes the 'man upstairs' attitude towards God and replaces it with a Biblical understanding of the 'Fear of the Lord'.

This insight and obedience to its truth will inspire and energize our daily walk with God and open the way for unprecedented harvest in our churches, communities and nations in the 21st century.

Ian & Pauline Cole
World Prayer Centre, Birmingham, UK

In an age where truth is suppressed, evil is rampant, sin is glorified and the wicked are seemingly prevailing, it is so refreshing to see a clear roadmap back to where we belong as the Church.

Written as a clarion call for our day, *In Holy Fear* draws us back to the truth once handed down, and is a level–headed push into the Spirit of the Fear of the Lord, which has gripped the hearts of thousands in historic revivals. What a great reminder of the fact that the Fear of the Lord (more than just respectful awe) actively permeates the Scripture from Genesis to Revelation! It's time to get off the detours of distraction and back on the highway of holiness where the Fear of the Lord is greater than every other fear!

Seriously, this book has the potential to release a whole new move of the Spirit, not only in your own life, but also in those around you as it's a great study book for small groups as well!

Rick Barker
Senior Pastor, Cariboo Christian Life Fellowship, BC, Canada

We thank God for Alistair Petrie and this teaching and receive him as a gift from God to the body of Christ for this hour in our nation and the world. Alistair's understanding of the *true* Fear of the Lord and his clear teaching on this subject adds another dimension of authority to those who are deeply committed to seeing communities and entire regions released from the death grip of an unrelenting enemy. Our SWAT TEAMS will absolutely be applying this teaching to our arsenal of strategies, as we train up God's people who desire to see the power and presence of God invade their territories. This book really brings to life the Scripture in Deuteronomy 11:25, "No man shall be able to stand against you; the Lord your God will put the dread of you and the fear of you upon all the land where you tread, just as He has said to you."

Dr Ivan and Linda Doxtator
Directors of First Nations Counseling Ministries — Canada

Some books are like thin, clear, consommé soup. Pleasant, light and gentle on the palate. This book is like a rich thick meaty soup.

Every chapter, nay at times every page, is so rich in information and revelation that you often have to pause and digest before moving on. I thought I was well informed on the fear of the Lord before I read the book, but as I moved from chapter to chapter I realized that I was still paddling in the shallows. If you are a gatherer of powerful sentences as memorable quotes this is a book with deep pockets. Keep a pen and paper handy. Highly recommended for the serious disciple.

Ken Symington
International Bible teacher, Author,
Founder of Christian Restoration in Ireland, UK

The book in your hands represents much more than a single body of thought or a string of biblical ideas. This material represents the lifestyle of its author, a desire for authentic revival as well as "a word in due season". Dr. Petrie never skims the surface. The thoughts go deep beneath the veneer of casual Christianity, lifting the veil of lawlessness to reclaim a healthy respect for the presence of God. I love the current message with both historic accuracy and biblical authenticity.

Read it, then read it slowly with a hi–lighter, then read it again. It will stir you, as it should. Thank you Alistair for your quest to go deeper and take us with you.

Lorne Tebbut
Senior Minister and Founder of C3 Calgary West,
Regional Overseer of C3 Canada

My friend Alistair Petrie is an amazing and anointed gift to the Body of Christ. His ability to take spiritual truth and give application to that truth is simply uncanny. The concept of the "Fear of the Lord" is almost lost in much of our modern church culture today, yet it is a vital component of true biblical awakening, revival and transformation.

The examples of transformation in this book will inspire you and build your faith. I pray the principles shared in this book will help you experience an authentic move of the Holy Spirit, not only in your personal life but in your communities, cities and regions. TO GOD BE THE GLORY!

Doug Abner
Appalachian Centre for Transformation

Compelling, vital and a wakeup call….

In a business world filled with chaotic and disruptive change, wisdom and understanding are needed more than ever. To truly have a Kingdom business to fulfil the Lord's purpose, it is more than just having business methodologies and Christian principles for success, it is also having a 'Fear of the Lord' and an intimate relationship with God that flows through into every aspect of your business.

Through every sentence, paragraph and chapter, Alistair has woven this message on a sound theological foundation with great practical insight and current experiences. This book is vital for the days ahead, and indeed the days we are in right now. It is a book that needs to be read and re–read so that its richness permeates deep into your spirit. The practical guidance is invaluable.

David & Margaret O'Connor
O'Connors Strata & Property Specialists;
Apartment Building Management Company, Sydney, Australia

This is a significant and transforming book! Alistair Petrie has distilled down in this straightforward no nonsense practical book one of the primary keys to the Kingdom of God. I have not found before such a clear presentation in any reading on this subject. In this book, Alistair Petrie has lifted off the veil and clarified the significance of the Fear of the Lord!

I found that I had to re–read much of it because of the revelation it has brought to me. It has exposed false perceptions to me and has given me much excitement and hope as a result. This book reflects the clarity and personal intensity of the author to bring truth to each of us in a straight forward practical understanding. This author is worthy of your investment!

Alexander Morrison
Director, Ellel Ministries Western Canada

Praise God for the opportunity I have had to read and review *In Holy Fear*. Before reading this book I did not have respect for the importance of the 'Fear the Lord' as I do now.

The book is an excellent illustration of how fear of the Lord connects with our view of God and our readiness to stand in the gap for Jesus. For us, the Fear of the Lord means to humble ourselves before the Lord as we steward *Peddie Roofing*. Just recently I went through a period of fear (relating to cash flow in the business) and as I humbled myself before the Lord, the Lord revealed active roof projects I was able to invoice and then receive immediate payment.

This book is a blessing and I look forward to taking more time to read it. The book has encouraged me to take up my cross and follow Jesus!

David Peddie
President and CEO, Peddie Roofing, Calgary, Alberta, Canada

ACKNOWLEDGEMENTS

This book has been on my personal "to do" list for many years. However in the past season, I have sensed the Lord asking me to write it with increasing urgency. Many have encouraged me in this journey — especially my wife Marie who has given me the space and time to disappear into the basement and to place in writing what has been burning on my heart for many years. Her prayers and love and support have been quite profound!

I also want to acknowledgment the encouragement of our sons Mike and Richard and their wives Damaris and Anna. They, and our grandchildren, are a joy to Marie and me, especially since they also continue to learn what it means to walk and live in the Fear of the Lord. Their prayers for us have been amazing.

Our Board members have also encouraged me immensely — Bob and Gini and Rick and his wife Marci, along with dear friends who have walked with us for years — Lance and Jill, Larry and Sheryl, Ray and Arlene, Steve and Nancy, Peter and Fi, Dave and Margaret, Errol and Helen, Ruth, Kathleen, Lorrie and countless others.

Jim and Jeannie Rodgers have spent hours listening to my voice on tapes and Jeannie has been outstanding in transcribing the initial manuscript. Sid and Cheryl Molenaar have given us endless support, and Cheryl has been amazing in the way she has patiently taken me through an initial but thorough editing process. That is the part of writing I do not enjoy! Thank you so much Cheryl.

But it is to the Lord Jesus I give utmost thanks who has taken me through all these experiences that lie behind the pages of the book and which bring to life the power of Scripture. May He be the One who receives all honor and glory in whatever way this book will be a witness to His call and challenge to the Church in the twenty–first century.

DEDICATION

Pursuing the Fear of the Lord has been a passion for me throughout my years as a Christian. It seems to me that the years are passing quickly and I am more aware of the brevity of life than ever before. It is my hope and fervent desire to finish well in all that the Lord has placed on my heart ever since I first encountered Him many years ago. I can honestly say He has never let me down nor has He ever forsaken me — even when at times my humanity has had other thoughts! Thank You, Lord — this book is all about You — and it is for You.

Psalm 128 is all about the benefits of understanding and living out the Fear of the Lord. It is a Psalm that should be carefully studied and prayed through regularly. The promises for families are quite amazing — with blessing, prosperity, and fruitfulness being part of the "fruit". I have watched my sons become Dads each in their own way — distinctive and unique — but what I love is the manner in which they model the love of the Lord for their children. For me, Mike and Richard are — as the Psalmist promised — like olive shoots. I have lived to see their children begin to blossom and grow and, already for Elijah and Benjamin, as well as Daniel and Gabriella, the legacy of the Lord is bearing much fruit. So to my sons and your wives, Damaris and Anna, keep walking in the Fear of the Lord. You will always encounter the Lord's blessing, no matter what challenges you go through. I dedicate this book to you.

Little is being hidden from us in this day and age. The horrors and atrocities we see and hear are ubiquitous. We could easily walk in the fear of what is going on around us thinking there is no hope. Yet the Psalmist puts it this way — "I will instruct you and teach you in the way you should go; I will counsel you and watch over you." (Psalm 32:8) What an incredible promise. That is what the fear of the Lord is all about.

We are all on a journey in this day and age but the Author and Perfecter of our faith has gone ahead of us. It was God's faithfulness in his life that enabled Paul to write these words in Philippians 1:6 — "being confident of this, that He who began a good work in you will carry it on to completion until the day of Christ Jesus."

That promise is also for you and me. The best is yet to come. Let's get started!

Alistair P. Petrie
Kelowna, BC — 2015

CHI–Books
PO Box 6462
Upper Mt Gravatt, Brisbane
QLD 4122
Australia

www.chibooks.org
publisher@chibooks.org

In Holy Fear — *Rediscovering the Fear of the Lord*

Print ISBN: 978-0-9942607-2-7
eBook ISBN: 978-0-9942607-3-4

Printed in Australia, United Kingdom and the United States of America.

Distributed in the USA and Internationally by Ingram Book Group and Amazon.

Also available from: Bookdeposity.co.uk and others like Koorong.com (AUS).

Distribution of eBook version: Amazon Kindle, Apple iBooks, Koorong.com and others like Wesley Owen (UK), Barnes & Nobel NOOK, Sony eReader and KOBO.

Editorial assistance: Anne Hamilton
Cover design: Dave Stone
Layout: Jonathan Gould

FOREWORD by Ruth Ruibal

This book wonderfully addresses one of the most important and challenging, yet seldom taught, issues the church desperately needs today. The nations are shaking and every aspect of life seems to be challenged or is crumbling before our eyes. The fear of man is prevalent not only in the world but in the church, and there seems to be no safe place left. As Alistair points out so well in his book, the fear of man has taken over most people, and the only remedy is the fear of God. But what is the fear of God? Where does it come from? How do we develop it?

I have had the privilege of traveling and ministering with Alistair and his wife Marie during the last decade but, of all the messages, to me this is the most challenging, as it brings us back to the most fundamental need for all mankind: the fear of God. Without it we are lost.

The church talks about desiring the transformation of our cities, regions and nations. However I haven't heard the fear of God being presented as a crucial ingredient for seeing that transformation nor, after seeing a degree of transformation, for maintaining it. We are in the most crucial time in history and one of the most important ingredients — the catalyst for change and seeing "Thy kingdom come, Thy will be done" is missing in our message! It is time to rediscover the fear of the God in order to be able to carry out His will in this "perverse generation".

All too often we hear about someone in the ministry who has fallen into sin. Some may think that perhaps they didn't really know the Lord and, although that may be true in some instances (Matthew 7:23), there are enough testimonies about their lives that it becomes obvious that the person was a genuine soldier of the Cross and has had a devastating fall. We ask ourselves what happened; it is hard to wrap our minds around it all. Again the essential, but missing, ingredient is the fear of God that is necessary for victorious spiritual warfare, as Alistair explains so well.

Although the fear of God can easily be traced throughout the Bible in both Testaments as well as in history in general, it is something that is usually misunderstood. In this book, Alistair gives a clear and challenging definition of the fear of God and the balance between love and fear. He shows its importance not only in the transformation process of cities, regions and nations, but also in business, redeeming land and in all areas of our lives. He shows how the fear of the Lord results in intimacy with God and allows us to be part of that company who know their God and "will be strong and do exploits" (Daniel 11:32b KJV). It is an exceptional book that I know I will read many times because it is so impacting, challenging and, for me, life–giving and life–changing, and I am sure you will feel the same.

Dr. Ruth Ruibal
President, Julio C. Ruibal Ministries

FOREWORD BY PETER HORROBIN

A few years ago I resolved to read right through the Psalms on my annual holiday. I never got beyond verse 14 of Psalm 25. As I read the words, *"The Lord confides in those who fear Him; He makes His covenant known to them,"* I was suddenly gripped by a revelation that has never left me to this day.

The revelation was that there is only one master key to knowing the will of God — the fear of the Lord. I began to study every Scripture that referred to the fear of the Lord and discovered that it was the key to just about everything! Even Noah built the ark in holy fear (Hebrews 11:7). God confided in Noah because Noah was a man who truly feared the Lord. God gave him the details of His plan to save the human race and because of Noah's obedience we're alive today! Living in the fear of the Lord can have world–changing consequences!

For years now I have been wanting to write a book on the fear of the Lord! But thanks to Alistair Petrie I can tick that off my list of things to do before I die — for Alistair has now done it — and in a far better way than I could ever have done. I am deeply grateful to him for presenting to the Body of Christ a very readable treatise on what I consider to be the most important subject that today's church needs to rediscover the meaning of.

This fear is not quaking in fear before a terrible tyrant, but the deepest of deep awareness that our loving God is everything, that we owe everything we are to Him and that without Him we are nothing. It is because of Him that we have life and, only in and through Him, that we can live. Holy fear tunes our inner ears into the voice of God. In these severely testing days we need to hear Him above every other voice. His is the only voice that can be trusted. Exodus 20:20 also tells us that it is the fear of the Lord that will keep us from sinning.

If the fear of the Lord means that we will hear the voice of God guiding us and we will be kept from sinning, then there can be no doubt every single believer needs to know and understand what this important book is all about.

I urge you to get it, read it and live it!

Peter Horrobin
Founder and Director of Ellel Ministries International

TABLE OF CONTENTS

INTRODUCTION

FEAR ABOUNDS

We all have significant moments that stand out in our memories that may last for years, if not a lifetime. Many years ago I went to a dentist who dropped a tool down my throat by mistake. I almost choked to death! Obviously, it was more than an unpleasant experience and I responded by not going near a dentist again for many years. I experienced a form of fear that in fact traumatized me. Thankfully, over the years, I was able to rekindle my relationship with dentists, and I do visit them nowadays for routine check–ups.

On another occasion, I was travelling home from a ministry venue overseas. Part of my return itinerary necessitated my going through yet another foreign country. I was only transiting the airport but did not have a boarding pass for my next flight. I went to speak with one of the guards in that airport who immediately marched me down to a security office. I was harshly interrogated and traumatized by a group of security guards. My luggage was removed from the aircraft, and although I could not speak their language — I knew that I was in trouble! To say I was fearful was an understatement and it was only later that I was told that these guards had authority to shoot on sight before asking any questions. This all took place within the confines of an airport, yet others who were watching me were helpless to intervene. Had it not been for a miraculous intervention from the Lord, I may not have left that nation alive. That experience formed real fear in my life — although a different form of fear than that of visiting the dentist.

HOLY FEAR

On the very day when I became a Christian, I experienced another form of fear. In my earlier days in broadcasting, we were trained to be very pragmatic and to believe only in what we could see and analyze and rationalize with human understanding. The circumstances at that time led me to getting on my knees and asking the Lord to reveal Himself to me if He really was who the Bible said he was. Within seconds, a profound presence enveloped the entire room and, literally for many hours, I was on my knees and my face with my eyes tightly closed. I was certain that if I opened my eyes I would see the Lord Himself. Yet, at the same time there was a fear within me but not the same type of fear that I had had visiting the dentist or going through that airport ordeal. This was an entirely different form of fear — not one that I could readily understand — nor one that I could readily run away from. It simply embraced and enfolded me, gave me a sense of utter security, and removed all my uncertainties and concerns that I was going through at the time. It also strangely warmed me, highlighting my finiteness, but also the infiniteness of this 'heavenly presence'. Indeed, I had encountered the holy fear of the Lord, something that would change the rest of my life forever!

THE SHAKINGS ARE ON THE INCREASE

We are living in extraordinary days. Nothing is as it was even five years ago. Today, news reports of global events, good and bad, are available to us almost instantaneously as they occur. In 2013, *God's Design for Challenging Times* [1] — was published in which the first section was entitled 'God's Redemptive Shakings'. In that book I outlined what is meant by 'God's redemptive shakings' as far as the signs of the times are concerned. I outlined a template by which to discern and decipher what is currently happening in the global arena that affects us at virtually every level of life — politics — economics — morals and ethics — finances — as well as what is going on in the Church.

Since that book was published, these various signs of the times have continued to increase. It is so important the church today is aware of what is going on around us from God's perspective, so that we can be as relevant and urgent as possible in our call as the prophetic mouthpiece of the Lord.

MANDATORY — NOT OPTIONAL

The intent of this book is to rediscover the fear of the Lord in the 21st century. Many years have passed since the Lord first met with me in that profound encounter in my room. Over the years He has taken me on many adventures into many parts of the world. It has been an amazing journey being able to chronicle the various ways in which he has met with leaders of nations and cities and churches and businesses, when those leaders in a similar way asked the Lord to reveal Himself to them. Indeed, as I have researched historical revivals and what today we would call "templates of authentic transformation" right up to this moment in history, the common denominator in almost every circumstance is that the fear of the Lord was always a non–negotiable component in terms of God moving in the midst of His people.

This book is to remind us concerning this key part of God's character that He longs to share with His people. This cannot be considered as an "add–on" or optional extra. In every translation from the original text, Psalm 25:14 is totally profound in its message — "*The Lord confides in those who fear him; He makes his covenant known to them."* In other words, to the degree that we fear the Lord, He in turn will confide to us what is on His heart. Imagine the creator God confiding in the likes of you and me! It goes beyond human understanding. Yet, if this verse is true, there is something about the nature and character of God tied in with the fear of the Lord, that is absolutely essential in our understanding of His intent and love for you and me.

THE BREVITY OF TIME

During the chapters that follow, we will examine the fear of the Lord, and look at examples of what it means to have His fear in our midst — both historically and in contemporary settings. We will examine the fear of man and see why it is such a snare for the people of God.

We will also see what it means to pray in the power of the opposite spirit. There are several examples of this in Scripture, and it is an essential tool in our arsenal if we want to be deploying the weapons of our warfare in a tangible and comprehensive manner. Thus we steward what God entrusts to us, and see His boundary lines of influence extend within our area of responsibility. While we made reference to this in the book *God's Design for Challenging Times2,* (Chapters 4 & 5) we are going to examine the power and strategy and timing of the Lord when it comes to praying in the opposite spirit under the direction of the fear of the Lord. No matter what the challenge might be that is facing us or our church, our business or our city, there is always a way through even the most impossible of situations. This passage in the end furthers the extension of the Kingdom of God.

Through Scripture, we will look in depth at the benefits of having the fear of the Lord in our midst and why this is such a catalyst of change for communities and cities. We will cite examples of people in business who have invited the fear of the Lord into the complexity of their work life, and then who have witnessed a Kingdom business come into being in which the rule and reign of God encompasses all that goes on in that particular enterprise.

We will explain practical ways of applying the fear of the Lord in our own lives, as well as in our churches, our cities, and even our nations. This will include understanding how a stronghold or a shroud can affect an entire community or organization, and how this can be addressed through instructive and carefully prepared prophetic acts of prayer to establish the canopy of the Lord in that area.

As a ministry, we have been teaching on the subject of community transformation for many years. During this time the Lord has shown us numerous ways in which, if the fear of the Lord is prayed into an area under His direction and without any sense of manipulation or false expectation (fantasy thinking), then we should expect to see His fear begin to embrace that area.

The world as we know it is being shaken at this time. Horrific acts of terrorism seem to be on the increase at an astonishing rate within the global arena. Yet, the Lord is asking His people to focus in on Him, who has all authority in heaven and on earth. He wants us to embrace *His fear* irrespective of what human fears and traumas and uncertainties we may be going through.

As I observe and research and pray into current–day events, I am reminded of the sobering scripture found in John 9:4 — *"As long as it is day, we must do the work of Him who sent Me. Night is coming, when no one can work."* I am conscious of the brevity of time.

Proverbs 9:10–11 states — *"The fear of the Lord is the beginning of wisdom, and knowledge of the Holy One is understanding."* My purpose in writing this book, and my prayer for all who read it is that we emerge with a fresh understanding of wisdom and insight and know what it is to experience the fear of the Lord in the 21st century. I pray too that we come to understand how to pray that fear into being in a manner that will open up the eyes of cities and nations before the return of the Lord.

CHAPTER 1

A TIME FOR VIGILANCE

DARWIN, AUSTRALIA

During one of our visits to Australia, my wife Marie and I had the privilege of visiting the city of Darwin. Prior to touring the city, we visited Kakadu National Park, a vast territory with enormous beauty and diverse wildlife, but which is also a fairly hostile terrain. Our guide herself had once been venomized by a poisonous snake. Obviously she lived to tell us of the ordeal. It was indeed a testimony about survival in a very challenging situation. At one point she showed us an area of water full of crocodiles. Even though we did not always see them, they saw us! She relayed a story about one of her colleagues who was quite familiar with the territory and had guided many tours in that terrain. He had become somewhat complacent because, although he knew the crocodiles were there, they had not bothered him — at least not up until that point.

One day, while he was leading a tour, one of the members of his group cast a lure into the water and it became stuck in the reeds. When the guide went to retrieve it, a crocodile lunged out of the water and grabbed him, taking him to his death. Crocodiles, we were told, can memorize the activities of their intended prey for up to 4 months! Therefore, one needs to know well the lay of the land when going into such hostile terrain. There was immense beauty in that place, yet, within the splendour, there was also impending danger.

The following day we had a fairly intensive tour of Darwin. It has a compelling history. On the morning of 19 February, 1942, Darwin was routinely involved in day–to–day activities. At that time, approximately 45 ships were moored in the harbour. Suddenly, just before 10 a.m., a first wave of 188 Japanese bombers unleashed their deadly cargo on the harbour. Launched from four aircraft carriers located midway between Timor and Darwin, they targeted ships, personnel, the town centre and the wharf.

No response plan had been prepared in the event of an air raid. Ironically, these very aircraft had also been used to attack Pearl Harbour ten weeks before — but on this occasion they dropped more than twice as many bombs on Darwin. This was the first time bombs were ever dropped on Australian soil. For the next 42 minutes, the city continued to be under fire with devastating results.

Darwin was caught quite unprepared when the first bombs began to fall. A major part of the main wharf at Stokes Hill was destroyed, as well as much of the town area. After only two hours, a second force of 54 bombers attacked and severely damaged the Darwin RAAF base — the northernmost air force base in Australia. At least 292 people were killed and hundreds were wounded. Faced with the prospect of potential future attacks, many people left Darwin.

Why did this happen? Why were the military and the people of the land caught so unaware of this horrific invasion?

We learned first of all that, rather like the tour guide discussed earlier, a sense of complacency had prevailed. It was assumed and presumed unlikely that the enemy would attack the city. We read in the historical reports that Darwin's only air defense involved ten Kittyhawk aircraft and that their pilots had not previously seen combat. Other aircraft onsite were not yet serviceable at the time of the attack.

The defense was essentially unprepared, inexperienced and outmanoeuvred. As we further studied this invasion, we learned some very sobering details. While there were different forms of artillery available, the various crews who were to fire the anti–aircraft guns had received little training due to ammunition shortages.

A radar warning had been sent to the people in Darwin. But as the Darwin papers recorded, it was unsophisticated radar that was being used. When word was sent to Darwin that unidentified aircraft were travelling northwards — a trajectory cleverly used by the Japanese to disorientate the defenses in Darwin — the military did not believe it could be the Japanese. Instead they thought it would probably just be some American aircraft. As a result, air raid sirens at Darwin were not sounded before the raid, and only started after the initial attack had begun.

Consequently Darwin was poorly defended — in spite of its strategic importance to the defence of Australia. The Japanese inflicted substantial losses upon the Allied forces with little cost to themselves. Essential services such as water and electricity had been destroyed, creating an easy environment for looting and chaos. The consequences of all these oversights and insufficient preparation were immense — and to this day serve as an essential wakeup call both for the people of Australia, and also for all of us in the global arena.

BOMBED BUT NOT CONQUERED

As I pondered our time in Kakadu, and then our exposure to the history of Darwin, I personally felt such a quickening of the Lord in my spirit that the fear of the Lord came upon me. I sensed Him saying — *"This is the story of My church — it is totally unprepared — it has not read the terrain correctly — it does not understand the signs of the times — it does not understand the seriousness of the hour."*

It is not a time to be complacent — lethargic — blind to reality — unprepared — and certainly not a time to be ill–equipped for what lies ahead of us. As we observe what is currently escalating within the global arena, the church needs to understand its prophetic role in sounding the alarm. No one else has been given this responsibility.

What is important to note, however, is what was written on one of the historical signs in Darwin: "Darwin was a city that was bombed but not conquered." As a city, it was subject to several leadership errors causing a serious lack of preparedness. Today, it is a vastly transformed city yielding a reservoir of leadership insights.

IT'S TIME TO KEEP WATCH

In Matthew 25:1–13 we read about the parable of the ten virgins. Verse 13 says: "*Therefore keep watch, because you do not know the day or the hour.*" While the parable reminds us that we cannot purchase either more time or borrow someone else's anointing (their oil), we are warned to keep watch. The Greek word *gregoreuo* means to be vigilant, to be awake, to keep watch — not to become apathetic or complacent. As we learned from our trip to Kakadu, we must not allow ourselves to become neutralized by the environment and no longer keep watch on the terrain in which we live and work. The same warning is given in Revelation 3:2 with *gregoreuo* once again being used in this verse — "*Wake up! Strengthen what remains and is about to die, for I have not found your deeds complete in the sight of My God.*" These two verses indicate urgency and vigilance and sobriety in a time such as this.

A further warning is found in Romans 13:11 — "*And do this, understanding the present time. The hour has come for you to wake up from your slumber, because our salvation is nearer now than when we first believed.*" Here the Greek word that is used for the phrase "wake up" is *egeiro*[2], which means to be awake — to lift up — to lift out — to raise up — to rear up and even take up (for the sense of urgency).

In almost every historical account of authentic revival, people walking in the fear of the Lord have heard this urgency in their hearts to waken up and to respond to the seriousness of the hour on behalf of those who are asleep and ignorant or complacent concerning their response to the Lord.

In Scripture, the fear of the Lord is defined as the beginning of understanding. In other words, when we have understanding from God's perspective, this is in itself a wakeup call. With this understanding comes wisdom and knowledge and insight and direction and correction. Ponder these Scriptures:

> Proverbs 1:7 — "*The fear of the Lord is the beginning of knowledge, but fools despise wisdom and discipline.*"

Psalm 111:10 — *"The fear of the Lord is the beginning of wisdom; all who follow His precepts have good understanding."*

Proverbs 9:10 — *"The fear of the Lord is the beginning of wisdom, and knowledge of the Holy One is understanding."*

Job 23:13–16 — *"But He stands alone, and who can oppose Him? He does whatever He pleases. He carries out His decree against me, and many such plans He has still in store. That is why I am terrified before Him; when I think of all of this, I fear Him. God has made my heart faint; the Almighty has terrified me."*

Jeremiah 5:22 — *"Should you not fear Me?" declares the Lord. "Should you not tremble in My presence?"*

Psalm 2:11 — *"Serve the Lord with fear and rejoice with trembling."*

Psalm 19:9 — *"The fear of the Lord is pure, enduring forever."*

Psalm 33:8 — *"Let all the earth fear the Lord; let all the people of the world revere Him."*

Psalm 34:11 — *"Come, my children, listen to me; I will teach you the fear of the Lord."*

Psalm 86:11 — *"Teach me Your way, O Lord, and I will walk in Your truth; give me an undivided heart, that I may fear Your name."*

Ecclesiastes 12:13 — *"Now all has been heard; here is the conclusion of the matter: Fear God and keep His commandments, for this is the whole duty of man."*

THE FEAR OF THE LORD — INTIMIDATION OR INVITATION?

The fear of the Lord is much more than just having respect or reverence for the living God. The word 'fear' is used well over 300 times in reference to God. 1 John 4:18 says — *"There is no fear in love. But perfect love drives out fear..."* Therefore how can we, in fact, fear God while He drives out all fear? Is there a dichotomy in doing so?

> The fear of the Lord gives us perspective, reverence, awe, obedience to His Word, and the desire to resist evil.

Scriptures referring to the fear of God are derived from various Hebrew words such as *yir'ah*[3] (Psalm 2:11; 19:9; 34:11; Proverbs 1:7; 9:10) and *yare'*[3] (Psalm 33:8; 86:11; Ecclesiastes 12:13; Jeremiah 5:22). A further Hebrew word is *pachad*[4] (Job 23:15) which is translated as fear or terror or even dread.

In the 21st century, there has been a gradual diluting of the real meaning of the phrase "the fear of the Lord" into God becoming our "buddy", our companion, our friend in need, our colleague, or the God who is always in a good mood who hangs out in our hip pocket. While this may be somewhat of an overstatement, we will see in the following chapters that when people came together under the direction of the Lord and walked in His fear, entire communities became saturated with the presence and character of God. This is the creator God who tabernacles in the midst of His people. He is our friend; but He also is the creator God.

The fear of the Lord is only the beginning of wisdom. The great news is that the love of God, reflected through God's only self–revelation in the person of Jesus Christ, is also the God who gives us His power to cast out all human fear and to set us free from every form of bondage and lies.

> 1 John 4:18 — *"There is no fear in love. But perfect love drives out fear, because fear has to do with punishment. The one who fears is not made perfect in love."*

> John 15:12–13 — *"Love each other as I have loved you. Greater love has no one than this that he lay down his life for his friends."*

The fear of the Lord gives us perspective, reverence, awe, obedience to His Word, and the desire to resist evil, no matter how enticing it might be. But it also assures us of the love of God because the creator God Himself went to the Cross in the person of Jesus Christ and died for our sins and did what we could never do for ourselves (1 John 4:7–12). Paul is quite clear on this — *"But God demonstrates His own love for us in this: While we were still sinners, Christ died for us."* (Romans 5:8)

> The fear of the Lord is non–negotiable in order to be praying what is on the heart of God.

This is what establishes who we are in Christ.

As the Psalmist says in Psalm 118:4 — *"Let those who fear the Lord say: 'His love endures forever.'"* And the Psalmist also says in Psalm 147:11 — *"The Lord delights in those who fear Him, who put their hope in His unfailing love."*

The final book in the Bible puts it this way — *"Fear God and give Him glory, because the hour of His judgment has come. Worship Him who made the heavens, the earth, the sea and the springs of water."* (Revelation 14:7)

HE BEGINS WITH THE INDIVIDUAL

During these last few decades, our ministry has gone to various parts of the world chronicling what God is doing and encouraging the body of Christ in appropriating the fullness of God in their lives and in their areas of responsibility within society. Through informed prayer, God has clearly collaborated with His people when they are praying and releasing what is on His heart for these respective areas. While prayer is non–negotiable for the release of authentic transformation, similarly the fear of the Lord is non–negotiable in order to be praying what is on the heart of God (Psalm 25:14).

Praying what is on His heart is a prayer that will have significant impact in both heaven and on the earth. However, this type of prayer must start at the individual level before it can have any real impact at the corporate level. There must be a holy and pure motive for seeking the presence of the Lord in the first place, since we are standing in the gap on behalf of our cities and communities, and not purely praying for God to do collectively what we ourselves have not experienced personally. In other words, as individuals, we must first experience personally what we want our city or community to experience.

That is what gives credibility and tenacity to the cry of intercession in any community in order that the fear of the Lord is released and that God knows that we are willing to steward whatever He reveals and releases in our midst.

When we are praying in this manner, the Lord is directing us and informing us. This in turn will have a major effect upon the unity of the body of Christ in any particular area — no matter how large or small. The fear of the Lord enables us to determine what has occurred in a particular area where a breach between God and the people of the land may have taken place. Furthermore, it enables us to understand what breaches actually exist within that community at all levels of life, which may have given the enemy serious footholds in society (Ephesians 4:27).

We can see reality from God's point of view as we renew our minds to the mind of Christ (Romans 12:1–2; 1 Corinthians 2:16). Walking in the fear of the Lord in the way that God commands gives us extraordinary blueprint strategies right from the Lord Himself on how to access even the most impossible of situations that may confront us. It is *His* strategy that is being released, not simply just our strategy that we are asking God to bless.

OPENING THE EYES OF COMMUNITIES AND CITIES

Since the fear of the Lord is such an essential component in terms of understanding authentic community transformation, then it is the Lord Himself who will instruct us as to why any particular area is closed or blinded to the knowledge of His call upon their lives (2 Corinthians 4:4). When the corporate eyesight of a community is opened to the Lord, it is as if massive spiritual cataracts or scales are removed from the collective eyesight in that place. Then people can 'see' in a way they have never previously been able to. They can perceive the work of the Lord as never before. That is the moment when impediments and obstacles that have prevented earlier transforming revival from taking place can be addressed and removed. Such 'impediments' include pride and unbelief, offense, human sufficiency and various forms of distraction. They also include theological perspectives that have upheld belief systems that God was too sovereign or too abstract in order to meet with His people in such a fundamental and comprehensive manner.

While it may be challenging for people to believe that God really does have a destiny for communities and cities, the reminder of Acts 17:26–28 is compelling — *"From one man He made every nation of men, that they should inhabit the whole earth; and He determined the times set for them and the exact places where they should live. God did this so that men would seek Him and perhaps reach out for Him and find Him, though He is not far from each of us... 'We are His offspring.'"*

Proverbs 11:14 states: *"For lack of guidance a nation falls, but many advisers make victory sure."* In other words, the people of God (the church) become God's conduit for releasing His promises and direction and insight in that city or area. Consider these passages:

> Proverbs 11:10 assures us: *"When the righteous prosper, the city rejoices."*

> Proverbs 11:11 states: *"Through the blessing of the upright a city is exalted..."*

> Joshua 6:16 exclaims: *"... Shout! For the Lord has given you the city!"*

> Micah 6:9 reminds us: *"Listen! The Lord is calling to the city..."*

> Ecclesiastes 9:15 tells of the man who was poor by the world's standards but wise by the standards of God ...who saved the *city* by his wisdom.

> Matthew 21: 10 states that Jesus stirred the *city*.

> Mark 1:21 refers to the people of the *city* of Capernaum being amazed at his teaching.

CITIES RESPOND TO THE FEAR OF THE LORD

Scripture recounts several times in which people and even cities respond to the message of the Kingdom of God. In Acts 9:31 we read: "*The church throughout Judea, Galilee and Samaria enjoyed a time of peace… they grew in numbers, living in the fear of the Lord.*" Then immediately in the next passage we read of Peter ministering to the paralytic called Aeneas who is healed, which results in the two communities Lydda and Sharon turning to the Lord (Acts 9:35). This is the fear of the Lord at work in a tangible manner, affecting entire cities.

Jonah had to learn that obedience was part of understanding the fear of the Lord. Initially he ran from God's call upon his life to speak his message of repentance to the city of Nineveh. But when Jonah finally accepted God's call, the result was that over 120,000 people turned to the Lord (Jonah 3:10; 4:11). Obedience to the Word of God is key if we are to see the fear of the Lord released in our midst.

THERE IS INFLUENCE IN WHAT WE SAY

At times, we allow the fear of man to rule our decision–making and our emotions. In Jeremiah 18:11–12, God is speaking to His people about reforming their ways and their actions when they say, "'*It's no use. We will continue with our own plans; each of us will follow the stubbornness of his evil heart.*'" Similarly, Malachi 3:14 gives insight as to why we do not often see the reviving work of God in our midst on a more regular basis: "*You have said, 'It is futile to serve God. What did we gain by carrying out his requirements…?'*" Such a negative statement can actually paralyze people from praying for whatever God requires of His people. Yet in Malachi 3:16 we see what happened when just a few people embraced the fear of the Lord:

> "…*Then those who feared the Lord talked with each other, and the Lord listened and heard. A scroll of remembrance was written in His presence concerning those who feared the Lord and honored His name.*"

This is profound! The Lord will listen and hear and respond to those who enter into His fear and honor His call.

In Genesis 45:26, Jacob was told that his son Joseph was still alive. But we are told — *"Jacob was stunned; he did not believe them."* His spirit of grief was mixed with a spirit of unbelief due to the trauma of thinking his beloved Joseph was dead, and he could not even hear the truth. But then in verse 27, we read that when Jacob saw the carts that Joseph had sent with his brothers to carry his father back, *"the spirit of their father Jacob revived."* Even Zachariah (in Luke 1) was influenced by the power of the impossible and the negative thinking he had in believing his wife Elizabeth could never have a child. He did not believe the promise brought by the angel and so he lost the ability to speak (v 20) until his son was born. In other words, there was to be no more negative thinking and no more negative speech until the word of God was fulfilled!

> When we begin to pray the fear of the Lord over our communities, then we will see distinct and observable shifts taking place in society.

This is why it is so significant to allow ourselves to rest our case in whatever God has said. In Luke 1:28–30 the angel reminded Mary that the Lord was with her and she was not to be afraid. Luke 1:37 promises us that nothing is impossible with God. Jeremiah 32:17 says that nothing is too hard for God. In the same chapter, even the Lord himself says in verse 27: *"'I am the Lord, the God of all mankind. Is anything too hard for Me?'"*

As we will see in the pages that follow, when we begin to pray the fear of the Lord over our communities, then we will see distinct and observable shifts taking place in society. However, our challenge is to resist the opinion of man as well as the fear of man. These may try to distract us, disorientate us or dissuade us from praying the fear of the Lord into our midst.

THE KEY PRINCIPLE

Proverbs 9:10 reminds us: *"The fear of the Lord is the beginning of wisdom, and knowledge of the Holy One is understanding."* Both wisdom and understanding are key elements of entering into the fear of the Lord. Luke 11:52 reminds us: *"Woe to you experts in the law, because you have taken away the key to knowledge (the fear of the Lord). You yourselves have not entered, and you have hindered those who were entering."* Therefore, the fear of God is an impacting revelation of just how awesome and powerful and holy God really is. This is key to understanding the character and intent of God in our lives.

When Israel was rescued out of Egypt, God came to them and visited his people on Mount Sinai. Exodus 19:18 gives a graphic description –

> *"Mount Sinai was covered with smoke, because the Lord descended on it in fire. The smoke billowed up from it like smoke from a furnace, the whole mountain trembled violently."*

The response from the people was significant —

> *"When the people saw the thunder and lightning and heard the trumpet and saw the mountain in smoke they trembled with fear. They stayed at a distance and said to Moses, 'Speak to us yourself and we will listen. But do not have God speak to us or we will die.' Moses said to the people, 'Do not be afraid. God has come to test you, so that the fear of God will be with you to keep you from sinning.'"* (Exodus 20:18–20)

The fear of the Lord is all about His character and His holiness. When we have the fear of Lord at work in our lives, we are full of reverence and awe for who He is and we choose to be obedient even when it might be easier to fall into the trap of the fear of man. We make decisions to resist and reject evil. Moses tells the people that the Lord wants to establish *His* fear in their lives so that they will not sin (Exodus 20:20).

> *"What is the fear of God? The fear of God is the deep life–controlling sense of how dangerously holy, just, and righteous God is towards even the least of sinners. When you know God like this (dangerously holy)*

and when you know yourself like this (utterly sinful), this knowledge acts as a deterrent to sin since all sin is blatant rebellion against this God." (A.W. Tozer)[5]

THE INVITATION OF GOD

The fear of the Lord is not about being afraid that God is about to alienate someone. He does not come to destroy us. The true fear of God occurs when we are fully aware of who He really is, since then our own sinfulness and finiteness suddenly reveals our unworthiness to come into His presence. This is the significance of John 3:16 —

> *"For God so loved the world that He gave His one and only Son, that whoever believes in Him shall not perish but have eternal life."*

> John 17:3 states — *"Now this is eternal life: that they may know You, the only true God, and Jesus Christ, whom You have sent."*

> James 4:8 reminds us — *"Come (draw) near to God and He will come near to you. Wash your hands, you sinners, and purify your hearts, you double-minded."*

Here James is referring to the counsel Moses gave the people in the Old Testament.

> Hebrews 10:22 puts it this way —

> *"Let us draw near to God with a sincere heart in full assurance of faith, having our hearts sprinkled to cleanse us from a guilty conscience and having our bodies washed with pure water."*

The fear of the Lord is **His invitation** to us to draw near to Him with complete intimacy, and the assurance that He will cleanse us, refine us and complete us, and will prepare the way that is set before us.

By relating with us in this way, God is revealing how awesome and powerful He is in our lives in order that we will always have a healthy fear of Him and not want to sin against Him either in thought, word or deed. As the Psalmist puts it in Psalm 33:8 — *"Let all the earth fear the*

Lord; let all the people of the world revere Him. "This is the understanding of God in relationship with His people that is carried right on into the New Testament.

Similarly Paul says in 2 Corinthians 7:1 — "*Since we have these promises, dear friends, let us purify ourselves from everything that contaminates body and spirit, perfecting holiness out of reverence for God* (i.e. the fear of the Lord)." If we really do want to seek after genuine holiness in our lives, it can only be done when the Lord is our reference and we seek intentionally to apply the fear of the Lord in our lives.

In Ephesians 5:21, Paul instructs the believers in Ephesus: "*Submit to one another out of reverence for Christ.*" The New American Standard Bible[6] translates this as: "*And be subject to one another in the fear of Christ.*"

In his first epistle, Peter underlines this truth — "*Show proper respect to everyone: Love the brotherhood of believers, fear God, honor the king.*" (1 Peter 2:17)

As we already have seen as evidenced in Acts 9:31 — "*The church…was strengthened; and encouraged by the Holy Spirit, they grew in numbers, living in the fear of the Lord.*" We need to note that the fear of the Lord at work in His church resulted in the people being strengthened and encouraged, the church growing in numbers and a quality of life enjoyed by all.

Understanding and appropriating this in our lives is part of the mandate of the Gospel until the return of the Lord. Revelation 14:6–7 makes this clear — "*Then I saw another angel flying in midair, and he had the eternal gospel to proclaim to those who live on the earth — to every nation, tribe, language and people. He said in a loud voice, 'Fear God and give Him glory, because the hour of His judgement has come. Worship Him who made the heavens, the earth, the sea and the springs of water.'*"

JESUS AND THE FEAR OF GOD

In Matthew chapter 10, Jesus sends out His disciples in order to undertake some fieldwork. In the course of their training and learning on the job, Jesus makes a very distinct statement in verse 28 — "*Do not be afraid of those who kill the body but cannot kill the soul. Rather, be afraid of the One who can destroy both soul and body in hell."*

This means two things. First of all, we are not to fear man. We will look at this subject in the next chapter.

Secondly, we are to fear God. Jesus is saying that the fear of God is rooted in knowing His ability to judge and admonish, and even punish us, and

> A healthy fear knows that we will one day appear before the judgement seat of Christ.

that He alone holds the keys that can destroy both soul and body in hell. Therefore, we should be living our lives with a 'healthy fear' in which our understanding of God is not based on assumption or perception or even tradition. A healthy fear knows that we will one day appear before the judgement seat of Christ. For this reason, Paul says in Philippians 2:12–13 — *"Therefore, …continue to work out your salvation with fear and trembling, for it is God who works in you to will and to act according to His good purpose."*

In other words, we are to be aware that God is at work in our lives, and we should respond to what He is doing in us and through us with holy reverence and even trembling. We must never take God for granted. He is after all, the creator God. Even though we are given the gift of free will and choice, it is to our advantage not to disobey what He tells us to do, or alternatively to do what He has told us not to do.

THE FEAR OF THE LORD REVEALS HIS CHARACTER

There are well over 300 references to the fear of the Lord in the Bible. We have looked at just a few of these Scriptures and each has significance to the relationship of God with His people. They also reveal how we are to conduct business here on earth. Collectively therefore, if we place these different references together concerning the fear of the Lord, we will see three distinct emphases concerning His character in His relationship with us:

1. We are to be in awe of Him.

One of the most worrisome passages of Scripture can be found in Malachi 2:1–2 — *"And now this admonition is for you, O priests. If you do not listen, and if you do not set your heart to honor My name," says the Lord Almighty, "I will send a curse upon you, and I will curse your blessings. Yes, I have already cursed them, because you have not set your heart to honor Me."*

Then in verses 5–6 the Lord continues — *"My covenant was with him, a covenant of life and peace, and I gave them to him; this called for reverence and he revered Me and stood in awe of My name. True instruction was in his mouth and nothing false was found on his lips. He walked with Me in peace and uprightness, and turned many from sin."*

God gives very clear guidelines for His priests — but if we do not walk in a sense of reverence and awe, He will even curse our blessings! This is not something that can be taken lightly. If we try to dilute or minimize the fear of the Lord in our lives, then we cannot expect the full counsel of the Lord to work in and through us in the way that He would want.

2. We are to be obedient to Him.

As we have seen in the case with Jonah, the fear of the Lord also requires our being obedient even when we do not want to be obedient.

Acts 5:29 reminds us that — *"We must obey God rather than men!"* 1 John 5:3 states — *"This is love for God: to obey His commands. And His commands are not burdensome."* Jesus Himself says in John 14:23–24 — *"If anyone loves Me, he will obey My teaching. My Father will love him, and we will come to him and make our home with him. He who does not love Me will not obey My teaching."*

Deuteronomy 6:3 gives us a clue as to why the power of obedience is so important for the people of God. *"Hear, O Israel, and be careful to obey so that it may go well with you and that you may increase greatly in a land flowing with milk and honey, just as the Lord, the God of your fathers, promised you."*

In loving the Lord in this manner, we release His flow of direction, guidance, provision, nourishment, protection, correction and the fulfillment of His promises in the lives of His people.

3. We are to resist whatever He calls evil.

The fear of the Lord also creates in us a decision to hate evil and to reject what is wrong. Hebrews 10:31 states: *"It is a dreadful thing to fall into the hands of the living God."* The New English Translation[7] of that verse states: *"It is a terrifying thing to fall into the hands of the living God."* The Revised Standard Version[8] is quite clear: *"It is a fearful thing to fall into the hands of the living God."* This is in the context of ignoring or abusing the knowledge of truth that God has revealed to us and then denying it.

> While we are not to be intimidated by the presence of the Lord, neither are we to take His presence for granted.

Concerning the sinfulness of the wicked, Psalm 36:1 states: *"... There is no fear of God before his eyes."* This is a serious indictment against the people of God who choose to reject the love and protection of God in their lives. Proverbs 19:23 succinctly summarizes these insights in this one verse: *"The fear of the Lord leads to life: Then one rests content, untouched by trouble."* What a powerful promise from God to His people who walk and live and worship in His fear!

SONSHIP VS SLAVE MENTALITY

This is what lay behind the *'fear'* that I experienced on that day many years ago when the presence of the Lord so permeated the room I was in and where for many hours I encountered his presence in a way that would change my life forever. Up until that moment, I had known about God, having grown up in a church–based home, but had never 'known' Him in such an intimate, personal manner. I did not want to disobey or dishonour what was now becoming life–changing to me.

> 'Sonship fear' is God's way of motivating us to seek and please Him.

In the Hebrews 10:31 passage, the Greek work word *phoberos* (*from phobos*[9]) is being used so that the idea of terror or dread is understood by the reader. While we are not to be intimidated by the presence of the Lord, neither are we to take His presence for granted, and the use of *phobos* is the same as the Hebrew word referred to earlier — *Yir'ah*.[10] Consequently, if we are to grasp what Proverbs 1:7 refers to in saying that the fear of Lord is the beginning of knowledge, then we cannot take lightly what it means to be in the hands of the loving God as revealed in the person of Jesus. This is essential if we are to understand what God–ordained revival involves. There needs to be a 'holy dread' so that our familiarity of God does not compromise His holiness.

This is not a fear based on intimidation — it is a fear based on absolute divine holiness and 'separateness'. This is what lies behind Exodus 20:18–21 in which we see the people full of fear and even trembling due to the presence of God experienced through the thunder, the lightning and the sound of the trumpet. Little wonder they stayed at a distance and asked Moses to be their go–between in conversing with this holy, powerful God. Moses already had experienced the presence of God and assured the people by saying: *"Do not be afraid. God has come to test you, so that the fear of God will be with you to keep you from sinning."*

Therefore, on the one hand the people were not to tremble in fear, yet on the other hand God had come to reveal Himself in such a profound manner so that they *would* fear Him and so keep His commandments. They were not to be *afraid* of God and be terrified to be in relationship with Him, but they were to fear Him as a deterrent to sin. They were not to become so familiar with God that they would lose His sense of infiniteness, and compromise this with their finiteness.

God was teaching His people not to fear Him in the way that slaves would fear their masters, but rather as sons; and yet not to take Him for granted. Slaves try to appease and please their masters in a different manner than sons who want to please and learn from their fathers. 'Sonship fear' is God's way of motivating us to seek and please Him. Jesus Himself models this in His relationship with the Father — *"I tell you the truth, the Son can do nothing by Himself; He can do only what He sees His Father doing, because whatever the Father does the Son also does."* (John 5:19) What is the benefit of this? Verse 20 states emphatically — *"For the Father loves the son and shows Him all He does. Yes, to your amazement He will show Him even greater things than these."*

Jesus further underlines this level of intimacy and relationship in John 8:29 — *"The One who sent Me is with Me; He has not left Me alone, for I always do what pleases Him."* Jesus models what these early Old Testament Scriptures indicate: God wanted us to be in a 'Sonship' relationship with Him rather than in that 'slave mentality relationship' from which He rescued His people out of Egypt.

Isaiah 11:2–3 prophetically describes the relationship of Jesus with His Father — *"The Spirit of the Lord will rest on Him ....the Spirit of knowledge and of the fear of the Lord — and He will delight in the fear of the Lord."* Therefore, Jesus took delight in embracing the fear of the Lord — a powerful model for His people.

Just as Moses pursued the fear of the Lord (Exodus 19–20) and experienced the holiness of God, so also Paul appeals to the body of Christ to have a similar desire in their relationship with Him:

> *"...As God has said: 'I will live with them and walk among them, and I will be their God, and they will be My people.' 'Therefore come out from them and be separate,' says the Lord. 'Touch no unclean thing, and I will receive you. I will be a Father to you, and you will be My sons and daughters...' Since we have these promises, dear friends, let us purify ourselves from everything that contaminates body and spirit, perfecting holiness out of reverence for God."* (2 Corinthians 6:16–7:1)

These are profound words from Scripture that describe the relationship God wants to have with us, so that we, His children, can experience the

> We should want to fear God since we know that sin displeases Him.

fullness of His presence, His love and His holiness in our midst. Therefore we are to come out of any type of lifestyle that would be contrary to God's Word, because such a way of life removes His holiness from our midst. Paul is making the point that we should *want* to fear God since we know that sin displeases Him. If we love God, we will not want to incur His displeasure, and we should fear the fact that our love of sin could well be greater than our love of God.

GOD WANTS TO EMBRACE COMMUNITIES

This can become a powerful prayer that we can be praying over and around our communities on behalf of the rest of the people who live there. Case studies of historical revival have shown that when the fear of the Lord embraces a community, a sense of His holiness, justice and destiny is released. It is an expression of Isaiah 66:5 — "*Hear the word of the Lord, you who tremble at His word...*" This is what the Psalmist refers to in Psalm 2:11–12 — "*Serve the Lord with fear and rejoice with trembling. Kiss the Son* (which means to be in agreement with the Son) *lest He be angry and you be destroyed in your way....Blessed are all who take refuge in Him.*"

If the people of God themselves are not willing to experience this first, it substantially reduces any effectiveness our prayers can have for other people if we are wanting the Lord to embrace them with His holiness and His presence. The fear and awe of God that He looks for in His people is evidenced in Matthew 10:32–33.

> "*Whoever acknowledges Me before men, I will also acknowledge him before My Father in heaven. But whoever disowns Me before men, I will disown him before My Father in heaven.*"

GOD WANTS TO ACKNOWLEDGE US

Putting it another way, as we acknowledge Him, He acknowledges us. One of the most amazing verses in Scripture is found in Hebrews 11:16 —

"…. Therefore God is not ashamed to be called their God, for He has prepared a city for them." This means He will endorse us, ratify us, protect us and even proclaim us in the heavenlies. God is not ashamed to be called our God. He is, in effect, surnaming Himself after us. Isaiah 45:4 RSV[11] states — *"For the sake of My servant Jacob, and Israel My chosen, I call you by your name, I surname you though you do not know Me."*

This is extraordinary. God is identifying us with Him! In the intimacy of a relationship such as this, nothing can be concealed about us that will give the enemy any right of access or leverage in our lives. This minimizes the right of any foothold the enemy can place before us (Ephesians 4:27) and alerts us to any known or unknown sin that we may have that gives the accuser of the people of God the right to accuse them only two times — daytime and night–time! (Revelation 12:10) This becomes key in the manner in which we pray for our communities, our cities, our places of business and even our nations. When we fear the Lord in this manner, it removes any sense of fatalistic thinking, complacency or apathy on our part. It assures us that God will intervene in the issues of life to the degree that His people are standing in the gap with integrity, with tenacity, with authority, but also with a clear understanding of what the holiness of God fully represents.

Understanding God at this depth becomes a defining characteristic that lies behind our appropriating the keys of the Kingdom of heaven as referred to in Matthew 16:19. These 'keys of the Kingdom' are holy and powerful weapons that can change events in society so that God's Kingdom can be extended. This is the seriousness of the stewardship that God has entrusted to His people.

Ponder the amazing promise that God gives in John 14:12–14 — *"I tell you the truth, anyone who has faith in Me will do what I have been doing. He will do even greater things than these, because I am going to the Father. And I will do whatever you ask in My name, so that the Son may bring glory to the Father. You may ask Me for anything in My name, and I will do it."* The binding and loosing of God's purpose on earth has a significant and immediate cause–and–effect in heaven, as promised in his word.

BECOMING FRIENDS OF GOD

When we understand the fear of the Lord in this context, we actually become friends of God. We are able to discern His mind and know what is on His heart (1 Corinthians 2:16). This was the experience of many leaders in biblical days — Abraham, Moses, David, Joshua, Elijah, and Paul — all who were friends of God and who understood His mind and His heart — and who chose to embrace and seek His fear and holiness. It is the same promise for you and me! John 15:14–16 makes this abundantly clear —

> When the fear of the Lord begins to penetrate a community people in that area suddenly become highly aware of their humanity and their sinfulness before God.

"You are My friends if you do what I command. I no longer call you servants, because a servant does not know his master's business. Instead, I have called you friends, for everything that I learned from My Father I have made known to you. You did not choose Me, but I chose you and appointed you to go and bear fruit — fruit that will last. Then the Father will give you whatever you ask in My name."

As His friends, we can pick up His sword and divide the superficiality of life and society from the reality and the fullness of life that God wants for His people (Matthew 10:34–39). Jesus did not come to bring a temporary peace but a different type of peace not as the world gives, but one that releases the presence and holiness and purpose of God in our midst (John 14:27). When we utilize this sword, we are in effect utilizing the Word of God, which is living and active and sharper than any double-edged sword.

Hebrews 4:12–13 explains how this penetrates even to the dividing of soul and spirit:

"For the word of God is living and active. Sharper than any double-edged sword, it penetrates even to dividing soul and spirit, joints and marrow; it judges the thoughts and attitudes of the heart. Nothing in all creation is hidden from God's sight. Everything is uncovered and laid bare before the eyes of Him to whom we must give account."

Praying the fear of the Lord into our communities in this manner can result in the exposure of what is hidden and whatever gives the enemy his right of influence in our communities. When the fear of the Lord begins to penetrate a community, as is often evidenced in historical revival, the people in that area suddenly become highly aware of their humanity and their sinfulness before God.

In Exodus 33:13–17 the Lord assures Moses that He is pleased with him and knows him by name. What an extraordinary promise! The fear of the Lord is all about knowing the Lord in intimacy, in holiness, and in death. There is nothing superficial in His relationship with us. Then in Exodus 34:6–7 God explains His name to Moses: *"...The Lord, the Lord, the compassionate and gracious God, slow to anger, abounding in love and faithfulness, maintaining love to thousands, and forgiving wickedness, rebellion and sin. Yet He does not leave the guilty unpunished; He punishes the children and their children for the sin of the fathers to the third and fourth generation."*

Until we know the Lord with this depth of relationship and understanding, we are only in fact relating to Him in a superficial manner. Having the fear of the Lord is what constitutes **real authority** in our prayer life. When God reveals to us what is on His heart for any given circumstance, and we are praying *His prayer*, then He is in effect endorsing His word in and through us as we stand in the gap.

In other words, God actually asks us to work with Him in addressing the issues of life that confront humanity. He is approving what we are praying for. Consider James 5:17–18 — *"Elijah was a man just like us. He prayed earnestly that it would not rain, and it did not rain on the land for three and a half years. Again he prayed, and the heavens gave rain, and the earth produced its crops."* When God collaborates in and through us, He brings His purposes to pass, sometimes in miraculous ways.

Later in this book we will examine the many benefits that can be released within our cities and nations when the fear of the Lord is being released through the proper posture and prayers of His people in those areas.

However, we must first address a main adversary of the fear of the Lord in our lives, namely the **fear of man**!

CHAPTER 2

THE FEAR OF MAN IS A SNARE

A snare is a device often used in the trapping of wildlife. Normally it utilizes a cable formed into a loop and then suspended over a trail used by animals. As the animal enters the loop, it tightens the snare down on itself and it is captured by the neck or body. The creature is still alive and restrained, but it is possible for it to become entangled leading to fatal results.

Similarly, spiritual snares can become deadly entanglements for the people of God, especially when established through the fear of man. Consider various translations of Proverbs 29:25 on this subject:

> Proverbs 29:25 (NIV) — *"Fear of man will prove to be a snare, but whoever trusts in the Lord is kept safe."*

> Proverbs 29:25 (AMP) [1] — *"The fear of man brings a snare, but whoever leans on, trusts in, and puts his confidence in the Lord is safe and set on high."*

> Proverbs 29:25 (CEB) [2] — *"People are trapped by their fear of others; those who trust the Lord are secure."*

> Proverbs 29:25 (GNT) [3] — *"It is dangerous to be concerned with what others think of you, but if you trust the Lord, you are safe."*

> Proverbs 29:25 (MSG) [4] — *"The fear of human opinion disables; trusting in God protects you from that."*

When a person fears God, they are more likely to keep their word and reflect that quality in their relationships with other people.

It is clear from Scripture that fearing the Lord is good simply because it actually saves us from falling into the trap of our own sinful nature. When a person fears God, they are more likely to keep their word and reflect that quality in their relationships with other people. In preparing the material for this book, I circulated a question to various leaders around the world who have witnessed God at work in their lives, their ministries and in their businesses in a variety of different ways. I asked if they felt that praying the fear of the Lord had had any significant cause–and–effect in the changes that they have experienced. One pastor from my city, who is responsible for a large fellowship of people, responded to my question in this way:

"I do believe that the fear of the Lord is an issue that needs to come back on the table in Christian circles. I think that in our recent past many Christian leaders have avoided this topic for a few reasons:

a — We have been afraid of offending people

b — Many of the very broken people who come our way, deal with issues related to shame. At times I think that we are afraid that talking about the fear of the Lord might cause them to become 'afraid of God'.

c — We have become fearful of moving back into a form of legalism that many grew up with.

However, that being said, I do believe that we have been in danger of swinging too far in the direction of a 'Christ–less Cross' and a form of grace that allows people to feel they can live anyway they want. Thus, a new level of understanding of what it means to live with a 'healthy awareness' of the fear of the Lord is very necessary today."

Over the years we have worked with various organizations, churches and businesses in terms of seeking the fear of the Lord in their midst — when it would be so easy to be influenced by the systems of man and compromise the 'plumb line' of the Lord. Here is a testimony coming from the owners of a business in the Asia–Pacific region who manage many buildings, affecting the lives of thousands of people, and who have had to resist the fear and temptations of man on several occasions. I asked them what it meant to have the fear of the Lord at work in their midst and they responded:

> "*It is to have a reverence for God Himself and an awesomeness of His very character and nature. It is as though reverence and awe operate together on a foundation of love. When this revelation truly arrives deep in your spirit, it is your highest motivating factor and forms the foundation from which all decisions and actions are made. In the business arena particularly, we have been on a journey where every part of our being, especially our business skills, principles, logic, analytical tendencies, mathematical calculations, all five senses, preferences and fears, all bow to the Lord in reverence of who He is and our relationship with Him, and His will in every situation (sometimes, no matter how impromptu; illogical; inconvenient, expensive, etc., it might seem at the time.) It has been in those times that we have witnessed the power of God operating most powerfully.*
>
> *How remarkable it is that the creator of the universe, God himself, would desire a deep intimate relationship with each one of us. It is quite a journey to move from a theological understanding and appreciation of the fear of the Lord to an act of working out the reality of what this means in your day to day life and how you react, respond, make decisions, etc., it has been a journey of extreme trials but a journey that is unavoidable. It has been a journey of experiential reality... the journey continues.*"

It has, at times, been a costly decision for them to choose to become a company that made decisions based on the fear of the Lord, and not on the opinion or counsel of man. Having watched this company develop and expand in countless ways over the years has been a profound testimony in allowing the fear of the Lord to influence every aspect of company decision–making. As a result, this company has earned significant trust in large organizations that affect the entire nation in which they live and work. In making such a choice, however, we all need to be reminded of certain 'non–negotiables' in God's relationship and work with His people. More specifically, we need to know what God Himself resists, and even hates.

WHAT THE LORD HATES

Proverbs 6:16–19 outlines quite graphically those things that the Lord hates and detests. Even though the character of God is one of love and mercy and compassion and healing and forgiveness, nevertheless there are certain areas of our sinfulness that are detestable to God:

1. The Lord hates haughty eyes.

These are eyes that indicate pride and independence in people. These are people who give little or no reference to the Lord in their lives. These are people who work in the opposite spirit to that of the Holy Spirit, and do not seek first the Kingdom of God and His righteousness as we are instructed in Matthew 6:33. Haughty eyes are indicative of an independent spirit that is self–seeking, self–serving and one that determines its own destiny.

2. The Lord hates a lying tongue.

This is because a lying tongue will remove the parameters of God. God is a God of truth who brings revelation, insight and breakthrough. Jesus says in John 8:31–32 — "...*If you hold to My teaching, you are really My disciples. Then you will know the truth, and the truth will set you free.*" A lying tongue determines our own parameters for what is right and what is wrong. God makes this point abundantly clear in Isaiah 29:16 — "*You turn things upside down, as if the potter were thought to be like the clay! Shall what is formed say to him who formed it, 'He did not make me'? Can the pot say of the potter, 'He knows nothing'?*"

3. The Lord hates hands that shed innocent blood.

Numbers 35:33 gives clear direction from the Lord: "*Do not pollute the land where you are. Bloodshed pollutes the land, and atonement cannot be made for the land on which blood has been shed, except by the blood of the one who shed it. Do not defile the land where you live and where I dwell, for I, the Lord, dwell among the Israelites.*" Leviticus 17:11 states: "*For the life of a creature is in the blood, and I have given it to you to make atonement for yourselves on the altar; it is the blood that makes atonement for one's life.*"

Untimely bloodshed is one of the four major curses that affect the land — the other three being idolatry, immorality and broken covenants. The shedding of innocent blood is a disrespect for the God of life. Jesus Himself said in Matthew 23:35 — "*And so upon you will come all the righteous blood that has been shed on earth, from the blood of righteous Abel to the blood of Zechariah son of Berekiah, whom you murdered between the temple and the altar…*" Christ was the Lamb of God whose blood was shed to make atonement for our sins.

4. The Lord hates a heart that devises wicked schemes.

Psalm 86:11 says: "*Teach me Your way, O Lord, and I will walk in Your truth; give me an undivided heart, that I may fear Your name.*" 1 Samuel 16:7 puts it this way: "*…The Lord does not look at the things man looks at. Man looks at the outward appearance, but the Lord looks at the heart.*" He looks for leaders who are fashioned after His own heart (1 Samuel 13:14).

David said to his son Solomon: "*And you, my son Solomon, acknowledge the God of your father, and serve Him with wholehearted devotion and with a willing mind, for the Lord searches every heart and understands every motive behind the thoughts. If you seek Him, He will be found by you; but if you forsake Him, He will reject you forever.*" (1 Chronicles 28:9) It is in his heart that a man lays up and ponders the words of the Lord (Job 22:22).

Psalm 37:4 indicates that when we truly seek the desires of the Lord, then He will place His desires in our heart. Little wonder, then, that the cry of the psalmist in Psalm 51:10 states: "*Create in me a pure heart, O God, and renew a steadfast spirit within me.*" An undivided heart releases the strategies of the Lord, but a wicked heart is susceptible to the schemes of the enemy.

5. The Lord hates feet that are quick to rush into evil.

Again, the Psalmist would say in Psalm 119:105 — "*Your word is a lamp to my feet and a light for my path.*" In the same Psalm, note his prayer in verse 133 — "*Direct my footsteps according to Your word; let no sin rule over me.*" Proverbs 16:9 adds: "*In his heart a man plans his course, but the Lord determines his steps.*" The fear of the Lord determines the direction and the purpose and the timing of the Lord in our lives — but if we choose to jettison or ignore parameters, then our feet will be led by the fear of man and man's own judgement.

6. The Lord hates a false witness who pours out lies.

Jesus says in John 8:44 — "*You belong to your father, the devil, and you want to carry out your father's desires. He was a murderer from the beginning, not holding to the truth, for there is no truth in him. When he lies, he speaks his native language, for he is a liar and the father of lies.*" God hates lies because it is in total opposition to His character, the One who would lead us into all truth.

7. The Lord hates a man who stirs up dissension.

This is detestable in the eyes of the Lord and is in total opposition to the unity of the Godhead. Psalm 133 is a wonderful testimony to the power of living and working together in unity. As verse 3 indicates — "*… For there the Lord bestows His blessing, even life forevermore.*"

The prayer of Jesus in John 17:21–23 reveals the heart of God in this matter — "*…May they also be in Us so that the world may believe that You have sent Me…that they may be one as We are one: I in them and You in Me. May they be brought to complete unity to let the world know that You sent Me and have loved them even as You have loved Me.*" We are told in Acts 4:32 that all the believers were one in heart and mind. The power of praying together could cause even the place where they were meeting to be shaken (Acts 4:31).

Acts 9:31 states: *Then the church throughout Judea, Galilee and Samaria enjoyed a time of peace. It was strengthened; and encouraged by the Holy Spirit, they grew in numbers, living in the fear of the Lord.*" As the church moved and lived and worked and worshiped and prayed together, God was able to establish His purpose in the lives of His people. As a result, the message of the Kingdom of God began to spread.

Why does God hate these things? Because effectively, they eliminate what the Lord wants to do in and through us as His body, His friends and His prophetic mouthpiece on earth. He also hates those qualities because they are in total contradiction to His character, which He is constantly developing in each of our lives. Therefore, these issues, which reflect the fear of man, will eliminate the potential of God's transforming revival in our communities and in our cities.

As we have now seen, God hates it when the fear of man overrides the fear of the Lord. His very character and holiness—His direction, His provision, His protection, His inspiration, His miraculous intervention and even His correction are jeopardized when the fear of man trumps the fear of the Lord.

Concerning the sinfulness of the wicked, this is why the Psalmist says in Psalm 36:1–4 — "…*There is no fear of God before his eyes…he flatters himself too much to detect or hate his sin. The words of his mouth are wicked and deceitful; he has ceased to be wise and to do good. Even on his bed he plots evil; he commits himself to a sinful course and does not reject what is wrong.*"

And yet, conversely Proverbs 19:23 again reminds us: *"The fear of the Lord leads to life: Then one rests content, untouched by trouble."* What a remarkable and profound promise coming from the Lord Himself. It is similar to what Paul would later write in Philippians 2:13 — "…*for it is God who works in you to will and to act according to His good purpose."* Similarly in Colossians 3:3 — "…*and your life is now hidden with Christ in God."* No wonder Paul makes such a resounding declaration in Colossians 1:27 — *"To them God has chosen to make known among the Gentiles the glorious riches of this mystery, which is Christ in you, the hope of glory."*

CONSEQUENCES OF THE FEAR OF MAN

Life today often involves traps and snares, bondages and footholds that can cause us to resist the fear of the Lord, We are tempted to submit instead to a lesser authority found in the fear of man. There are several Biblical examples that reveal the consequences of falling into the snare of the fear of man.

A SET–UP THAT WAS ALMOST FATAL

In 2 Chronicles 17–20, we are given a graphic insight into the life of King Jehoshaphat. At the beginning of Chapter 18, we are told he has great wealth and honor but that he allied himself with Ahab, king of Israel, through marriage. In agreement these two kings went to battle against Ramoth Gilead. However, as the drama unfolds, Jehoshaphat almost loses his life by agreeing to the trickery of the evil king of Israel. God intervened and we are told in 2 Chronicles 19:2–3 — "...*Should you help the wicked and love those who hate the Lord? Because of this, the wrath of the Lord is upon you. There is, however, some good in you, for you have rid the land of the Asherah poles and have set your heart on seeking God.*"

Jehoshaphat turned the people of the land back to the Lord and his words to the judges of Judah in verse 6 are revealing: "*Consider carefully what you do, because you are not judging for man but for the Lord, who is with you whenever you give a verdict. Now let the fear of the Lord be upon you. Judge carefully, for with the Lord our God there is no injustice or partiality or bribery.*" In other words, when we work in the fear of man there can be injustice, partiality and even bribery.

Jehoshaphat then gives these orders in verses 9 and 10: "...*You must serve faithfully and wholeheartedly in the fear of the Lord...you are to warn them not to sin against the Lord; otherwise his wrath will come on you and your brothers. Do this, and you will not sin.*"

THE GOLDEN CALF

In Exodus 32 we have an account of the people of God who have been rescued out of Egypt. Moses was on Mount Sinai about to receive the commandments of the Lord. But the people grew restless waiting for his return. Aaron gave in to the fear of man and allowed a golden calf to be formed from the gold earrings of the people. In reality, God had delayed the return of Moses in order to test the hearts of His people so as to reveal the consumerism that still lay within their own hidden agendas. They were still tenderized to 'Baal–ism'. In reality, what is in the heart of humanity will eventually be exposed. God knew that, until these stumbling blocks and footholds were removed, His people would not be able to address the giants in the land they were about to enter. God allowed a climate of desperation to develop which, as we have seen in revival history, can lead to perseverance, which in turn leads to an awakening that occurs when the people enter into the fear of the Lord. This depth of desperation is not an option if we honestly want authentic transformation in our midst.

> The fear of man wants to redefine God in a way that is accessible and reduce Him to a safe place on our own terms.

Simply put, however, we will either worship God on His terms or our own idols on our terms. That is where the fear of the Lord must overcome the fear of man. The fear of man wants to redefine God in a way that is accessible and reduce Him to a safe place on our own terms. Consequently, God delays the release of His law, His glory and His chosen leader — in order for the people of God to become desperate for Him. It is in times of God's silence when the 'toxins' within us are released. When He is silent and when He delays, it is for a divine purpose that needs to be understood and received.

Amazingly, Aaron survived the judgement of God and he even tried to say to Moses: "'You know how prone these people are to evil.' They said to me, 'Make us gods who will go before us'... Then they gave me the gold, and I threw it into the fire, and out came this calf!" (Exodus 32:22–24) Three thousand people died that day because of their sin against God's holiness. The Lord himself even said to Moses: *"Whoever has sinned against Me I will blot out of My book."* (Exodus 32:33)

It was due to Moses standing in the gap on behalf of these people that the Lord relented and did not bring on the people the disaster that He had threatened. (Exodus 32:14). There were repercussions due to the fear of man that had affected the people and Aaron.

THE LIVING AND THE DEAD

In Numbers 16 we have a graphic description of the fear of man resulting in the death of many people. It was a case of Moses and Aaron standing between the living and the dead. (Numbers 16:48) We are told at the beginning of Numbers 16 that Korah, Dathan and Abiram became insolent and rose up against Moses (Numbers 16:1–2). Along with a further 250 leaders of the community, they opposed Moses and Aaron.

Fuelling their opposition were jealousy and an independent spirit. These caused lawlessness and a spirit of entitlement to develop. While they were Levites, they desired a certain level of recognition reserved only for the priesthood. Moses and Aaron intervened but not before a plague caused 14,700 people to die due to this insurrection of Korah and his followers. The fear of man can be very infectious which is why Moses warned the people in Numbers 16:26 — *"…Move back from the tents of these wicked men! Do not touch anything belonging to them, or you will be swept away because of all their sins…"*

God requires a separation between holiness and 'unholiness' in order that our motives and our relationships and our possessions are kept holy unto Him. Otherwise, this becomes the foundation upon which pride and idolatry grow, seducing humanity into the belief that it can be like God. This presumptuousness and self–inclined worship leads to idolatry, separation from God and ultimately, death. It is the call of the church today to stand between the living and the dead, which underlines the urgency of understanding the fear of the Lord being recovered in both the church and society today.

GIDEON — HIS TRAINING — HIS TRIUMPH — AND HIS TRAGEDY

In Judges 6–8 we have the remarkable story of Gideon. In Chapter 6 we are told of his unique training in the purposes and in the strategy of the Lord. Due to the fear of man, he is a shepherd threshing his wheat in a wine press. In other words, he is in the wrong place doing what he was supposed to be doing as a farmer. As God meets with him, Gideon prepares to cleanse the land of idolatry and offensive strongholds that the people had begun to worship. Gideon began to turn from the fear of man to the fear of the Lord. In Judges 6:23 the Lord says to him: *"...Peace! Do not be afraid. You are not going to die."* He was still afraid of his family and the men of the town (Judges 6:27) but in the end he became a leader full of the fear of the Lord (Judges 7:15–18).

In Judges 6:34 when the Spirit of the Lord comes upon Gideon, a good translation from the original Hebrew is that the Holy Spirit put Gideon on like a glove. Then, in Chapter 7 we have the amazing triumph of Gideon and his people in which 300 men defeat a vast army. It is an extraordinary victory that takes place.

However, in Judges 8:22–27 the fear of man reveals itself in Gideon once again. This time however, it takes another form. While Gideon is encouraged to rule over his people he responds correctly in verse 23: *"...I will not rule over you, nor will my son rule over you. The Lord will rule over you."* So far so good — then the improbable takes place. The fear of man rises up in the form of his acceptance of an earring from each one of his people. Along with other occultic objects taken from the defeated enemy, he fashioned the gold into an ephod, which he placed in his town of Ophrah. We are told that — *"All Israel prostituted themselves by worshiping it there, and it became a snare to Gideon and his family."* (Judges 8:27)

Although Gideon enjoyed peace for the duration of his life, this was not the case for his son Abimelek or for the Israelites. When Gideon died, the people once again prostituted themselves by committing idolatrous worship with Baal. Abimelek entered into a life of great sinfulness. The victory of the Lord through Gideon was not stewarded correctly and, as a result of the fear of man, the worship of the ephod became the downfall of the people.

In her book *Intimate Friendship with God,*[5] Joy Dawson states that:

> "*The fear of the Lord is the only way to be released from the fear of man. The fear of man is being more impressed with man's reaction to our actions than with God's reaction. That's bondage. When we have the fear of God upon us, we are impressed only with God's reaction. We are freed from the concern of what people think. That's freedom! That's release! That's great relief!*"

LESSONS FROM ANANIAS AND SAPPHIRA

In his book *The Fear of the Lord,* John Bevere[6] refers to the account of Ananias and Sapphira from Acts 5:1–11. This, in itself, is a fearful passage of Scripture because most people at one time or another could well see themselves in the same position as that of Ananias and Sapphira. In all probability this couple had been very faithful givers to the emerging church of the day. We are told in context (Acts 4:36–37) that Joseph had sold a field and brought the money and put it at the apostles' feet.

Let's remember that the Lord is a heart reader, not just a lip reader.

Ananias and Sapphira then did the same thing with a piece of property that they sold. They brought the money to the feet of the apostles, giving the impression they had offered all the proceeds for the purposes of the Lord when, in fact, they kept some of the money for themselves.

The drama unfolds when Peter questions both Ananias and then Sapphira on this issue and in Acts 5:9 — "*How could you agree to test the Spirit of the Lord?*" Let's remember that the Lord is a heart reader, not just a lip reader. In this particular circumstance, while they had given money for the work of the church, it was their heart issue that caused a deadly deception to occur, which led to their respective deaths. It is little wonder that — "*Great fear seized the whole church and all who heard about these events.*" (Acts 5:11)

Possibly different factors caused Ananias and Sapphira to fall into this snare of the fear of man, which led to their untimely demise. Possibly they wanted to have the appearance of being high–level givers or perhaps they wanted the praise and acknowledgement from the leadership of the church. Perhaps they had enjoyed earlier recognition from the entire Christian community and they were known as generous givers. Whatever their justification may have been, they compromised on the fear of the Lord and caved into the fear of man. They completely misunderstood what the holiness of the Lord actually involved. Bevere emphasizes this deep lesson when he says:

> "I'm sure Ananias and Sapphira were a part of those who were astonished and excited in the early church of Acts. All had been amazed by the abundant signs and wonders. Yet even signs and wonders will become commonplace when there is a lack of the fear of God in your hearts. The fear of God would have restrained the foolishness of this unfortunate couple. The fear would have revealed the holiness of God."[7]

Ananias and Sapphira chose to remove themselves from the cover of the fear of the Lord and rendered themselves vulnerable to the fear of man. The Psalmist puts it this way in Psalm 34:7–14 — "The angel of the Lord encamps around those who fear Him, and He delivers them… blessed is the man who takes refuge in Him. Fear the Lord, you His saints, for those who fear Him lack nothing… Those who seek the Lord lack no good thing… Whoever of you loves life and desires to see many good days, keep your tongue from evil and your lips from speaking lies. Turn from evil and do good; seek peace and pursue it."

LIVING A HOLY LIFE — PETER'S PRINCIPLE

In his first epistle, Peter also explains how to resist falling into the trap of the fear of man by explaining what it means to live a holy life. 1 Peter 1:15–18 — "But just as He who called you is holy, so be holy in all you do; for it is written: 'Be holy, because I am holy.' …live your lives as strangers here in reverent fear. For you know that it was not with perishable things such as silver *or gold that you were redeemed from the empty way of life handed down to you from your forefathers..."*

Bevere goes on to point out that the example made of Ananias and Sapphira had a profound effect upon the entire church at that time.

> *"Those who saw themselves in the irreverence of Ananias and Sapphira rent their hearts in repentance. Others counted the cost more seriously before joining themselves with the assembly of believers in Jerusalem. Some may have walked away in fear of God's judgement."* [8]

Yet, as Acts 5:14 indicates, people continued to be added to the membership of the church due to the power of holiness that pervaded the area. Signs and wonders followed as a result of this fear of the Lord coming upon the community. Again, to quote Bevere: *"In essence, Ananias and Sapphira fell over dead because they were irreverent in the presence of the Lord whose glory had been revealed already."* [9]

A PERSONAL SOBERING EXPERIENCE

On one occasion my son Michael and I were travelling together teaching at various venues in an overseas nation. Following one session, a woman came up to us with a sizeable sum of money and said, "This is for your ministry". Although I had a check in my spirit, I justified receiving this gift since it would be used for the extension of the Kingdom of God and, if there was any hidden agenda in the giving of these funds, it could easily be cleansed by prayer. I fell into the snare of man! Although the Holy Spirit immediately gave me a check in my spirit, I overruled that check! Thankfully, my son immediately looked at me and challenged my motive saying, "Dad, what are you doing?" I repented of taking the funds and immediately gave them back to the conference host and asked that he return them to the woman. I wanted to honor her gift to us and I wanted to justify receiving the funds for the needs of ministry. I resisted saying to her, right at that moment, that I felt the Lord did not want me to receive this gift. I was intimidated from speaking the truth.

This was the fear of man at work in me. Had these funds not been returned, our ministry would likely have come under a serious indictment from the

Lord and I would have been held responsible. At times we may receive gifts for the ministry coming from questionable sources. We know these gifts can be 'cleansed', however this is always subject to the scrutiny, direction and the final word of the Holy Spirit who knows what can be retained and what must be refused.

As we have already seen, Scripture is replete with examples of leaders who fell into the trap of the fear of man and resisted the fear of God, and thus paid the consequences. When they repented and turned back to the Lord, God was able to rescue them and taught them a serious lesson in 'earned authority' for their ongoing life and ministry. If they did not repent, they suffered the consequences because they were now trifling with the holiness of God. As Joy Dawson puts it,

> "It can cost us many things to fear God and not men – being misunderstood, the loss of friendships, closed doors in ministry, rejection of many kinds, persecution, and even life itself. It cost Zechariah and Stephen their lives to say what God told them to say, they feared God, not the people. The prophets Jeremiah, Micaiah, Hanani were all in prison for giving the word of the Lord. They feared God, not the people. Paul, Silas, and Peter were imprisoned for aggressively witnessing for Jesus Christ." [10]

The dilemma for every leader in pastoral responsibility is in resisting the pressure to say to people what they want to hear, rather than what they need to hear. As Dawson says, *"It is possible to have enough of the fear of God upon us to give the word of the Lord to the people with real authority and then to succumb to the fear of man after having given it."* [11]

I have often pondered the situation with Elijah who was involved in a dramatic encounter with pagan

> God's authority is released in and through us when we choose to be in submission and obedience to the Lord Jesus.

prophets on the top of Mount Carmel. When he came before the people, Elijah was bold in what he said: *"How long will you waiver between two opinions? If the Lord is God, follow Him; but if Baal is god, follow him."* God renders an amazing victory through His prophet, but then shortly after that Elijah flees to Horeb due to threatening words coming from Jezebel. So real was this fear in his life that as we read in 1 Kings 19:4 — *"…He came to a broom tree, got down under it and prayed that he might die."*

REAL AUTHORITY LIES IN PLEASING GOD — NOT MAN!

How important it is that we are more impressed with God than those that we encounter in the journey of life. Again, as Dawson puts it,

> *"Our ministries are marked with authority only to the degree that the life of the Lord Jesus is the only explanation of what comes forth from us. This is possible as we consciously, wilfully lean on the person of the Lord Jesus Christ in faith to do in us and through us what we are totally convinced we cannot do ourselves."* [12]

Paul reminds us in 1 Thessalonians 2:4 — *"On the contrary, we speak as men approved by God to be entrusted with the gospel. We are not trying to please men, but God, who tests our hearts…"* The Psalmist puts it in such a succinct way: *"I am a friend to all who fear You, to all who follow Your precepts."* (Psalm 119:63) That, in itself needs to be the litmus test that determines whether our relationships are under the fear of the Lord or under the fear of man.

God's authority is released in and through us when we choose to be in submission and obedience to the Lord Jesus — just as He was in His relationship with the Father. That is what releases the full resourcing of the kingdom of God in our lives and in our ministries — *"How great is Your goodness, which You have stored up for those who fear You, which You bestow in the sight of men on those who take refuge in You."* (Psalm 31:19)

When we resist the snare of succumbing to the fear of man, we become those who are more able to discern the heart, purpose, timing and authority of the Lord. This, in turn, is what will lead to a release of God's holy fear in our midst.

DUNCAN CAMPBELL AND THE REVIVAL IN THE HEBRIDES

Duncan Campbell, one of the catalysts during the revival in the Hebrides, commented on this holy fear in these words:

> *"I have known men out on the fields, others at their weaving looms, so overcome by this sense of God that they were found prostrate on the ground. Hear the words of one who felt the hand of God upon him: 'The grass beneath my feet and the rocks around me seemed to cry, flee to Christ for refuge.' This supernatural illumination of the Holy Spirit led many in (the Hebrides) revival to a saving knowledge of the Lord Jesus Christ before they came near to any meeting connected with the movement. I have no hesitation in saying that this awareness of God is the crying need of the church today. 'The fear of the Lord is the beginning of wisdom'; but this cannot be worked up by any human effort, it must come down."* [13]

It is through addressing the fear of man in our lives and ministries that we can prepare a community for the encounter of the fear of God, and this requires our entering into an understanding of what it means to minister in the **power of the opposite spirit**. This releases the kingdom of God in a manner that authenticates and demonstrates the activity of God in our midst.

CHAPTER 3

MINISTERING IN THE POWER
OF THE OPPOSITE SPIRIT

FROM HOSTILITY TO RECONCILIATION

A few months before writing this book, my wife and I were flying to another part of the country to speak at a conference. During the second flight we unwittingly sat in the wrong seats although our boarding passes seemed to indicate that we were seated correctly. We were just one row out of place and when a passenger mentioned this to my wife, she was willing to move, but he said not to worry, he would sit where she was supposed to be seated. However, the person whose seat I was occupying was not so accommodating and was extremely angry in his encounter with me. With a flight attendant and several people around him, he basically yelled at me and remonstrated me for what I had done. He was clearly very upset with me! During the duration of that flight, I realized that my emotions had been significantly challenged and it was somewhat hard for me to pray God's love upon that person!

Upon landing, we went to retrieve our luggage in the vast baggage area. The only people there were my wife, myself, and this person that had been very upset with me. Words do not aptly describe my deep emotion at that moment! It was then the Holy Spirit convicted me of my sinful response to his reaction. While initially I tried to justify my response before the Lord, He overruled and won. I found myself going to the man and apologizing and asking forgiveness for my having taken his seat. Initially, he resisted my apology but then he took my hand and realized I really was asking forgiveness. He was a businessman who probably had never had this happen to him before. As he looked at me his eyes turned from a glare to what was clearly a softening, confirmed by the manner in which he held my hand tightly. He looked at me and simply said, "Thank you". A few moments later after we had retrieved our luggage I turned around and he was gone. Suddenly I saw him at the far end of the baggage area and he turned and waved at me and left. He and I had gone from hostility to reconciliation in just a few moments.

> Any encounters we may have outside of the boundaries of the Word of God create shallowness and superficiality in spirituality.

In that brief encounter God had reminded me of a lesson that was not only important for what I was about to share at the conference, but also in the months following — in fact, right up to the preparation for this book. God is reminding His church about the importance of walking in the power of the opposite spirit and of recovering the fear of the Lord.

The paradox is that today many people in the church are being told there are new boundaries and new revelation available for the people of God; even beyond the boundaries of Scripture. We have made a fairly detailed study of this under the section of 'Deception in the 21st Century' in our book *God's Design for Challenging Times*.[1] This is a deadly deception because once we refer to new boundaries of revelation; we subtly remove the fear of God and instead factor in the fear of man. Can there honestly be a higher revelation than what is found in Scripture for revealing God's heart and holiness and His character to His people? Absolutely not! Any encounters we may have outside of the boundaries of the Word of God create shallowness and superficiality in spirituality. This is what compromises our lifestyles today and has created what can only be referred to as an increasing 'Cross–less Christianity' and a movement of hyper–

grace in which the 'yes' of God becomes our 'no', and His 'no' becomes our 'yes'. Consider these words from Isaiah 5:20–21:

> *"Woe to those who call evil good and good evil, who put darkness for light and light for darkness, who put bitter for sweet and sweet for bitter. Woe to those who are wise in their own eyes and clever in their own site."*

Years ago A.W. Tozer made a statement concerning the church of his day that has proven to have had prophetic accuracy for the times in which we now live:

> *"Religion today is not transforming people; rather it is being transformed by the people. It is not raising the moral level of society; it is descending to society's own level, and congratulating itself that it has scored a victory because society is smilingly accepting its surrender."* [2]

In *God's Design for Challenging Times* [3] we provide teaching on the subject of deception and boundary breaking in depth. Without the word of God as our solid foundation, there will be a continual and increasing shallowness in our morals and ethics, our convictions, and substantial compromise in our lifestyles. As Michael Brown puts it:

"…the believers understood that the One who sent His son to die for them and who gave them His spirit and now lived among them was holy, and He would not tolerate brazen acts of deception." [4]

As we learn how to live and move and work and worship in the fear of the Lord, so it is we increase our understanding of how to minister in the power and authenticity and authority of the Holy Spirit. This, in turn, alerts us to the subtleties of the opposite spirit that will attempt to engage us and try to defeat us, especially in this day of increasing deception. Paul puts it this way in 2 Corinthians 10:3–5 — *"For though we live in the world, we do not wage war as the world does. The weapons we fight with are not the weapons of the world. On the contrary, they have divine power to demolish strongholds. We demolish arguments and every pretention that sets itself up against the knowledge of God, and we take captive every thought to make it obedient to Christ."*

LOREN CUNNINGHAM

On one occasion Loren Cunningham, the founder of *Youth with a Mission*, was asked to comment on ministering in the power of the opposite spirit. His response was clear and concise:

> *"We were trying to buy a hotel and make it our campus in Kona. There was so much greed demonstrated because it was in bankruptcy court. I thought, 'O God, what do we do?' The Lord said, 'Minister in the opposite spirit.' That was a new phrase to me. I said, 'Well, what is the opposite of greed, Lord?' He said, 'Generosity.' Generosity! And I began to understand that walking like Jesus would walk destroys spiritual strongholds. It's talking like He would talk. Praying like He prays."* [5]

We have seen so far, that God revealed Himself to His people in the Old Testament days in order that they would fear Him and want to keep His commandments out of a love–based relationship, not out of a slave–based mentality. Therefore, they were encouraged to enter into a relationship with God based on intimacy and awe and obedience and the rejection of evil. Yet, at the same time they were to fear Him as a deterrent to sin and not to compromise evil for good as referred to in the Isaiah 5:20–21 passage quoted above.

THE FIERY FURNACE

Scripture contains many examples of people in Biblical days who, when faced with significant opposition and circumstances beyond their control, applied the principle of working in the opposite spirit and experienced the breakthrough of God. Consider the situation with Daniel, Shadrach, Meshach and Abednego as related in Daniel 3. They were faced with an impossible situation — either worship the image of King Nebuchadnezzar or be thrown into a fiery furnace. They chose to work in the opposite spirit and trusted in God and did not submit to the fear of man. In so doing they defied Nebuchadnezzar's challenge:

> *"…Then what God will be able to rescue you from my hand?"* (Daniel 3:15) This was outright mockery against God Himself. Then these

three young men went even further and clearly said: *"If we are thrown into the blazing furnace, the God we serve is able to save us from it, and He will rescue us from your hand, O king. But even if He does not, we want you to know, O king, that we will not serve your gods or worship the image of gold you have set up."* (Daniel 3:17–18)

God delivers Daniel, Shadrach, Meshach and Abednego in a miraculous fashion that resulted even in the king saying: *"Praise be to the God of Shadrach, Meshach and Abednego, who has sent His angel and rescued His servants! They trusted in Him and defied the king's command and were willing to give up their lives rather than serve or worship any god except their own God."* (Daniel 3:28)

As a result, Nebuchadnezzar declared that no one was to say anything against the god of these three men and declared: *"…no other god can save in this way."* (Daniel 3:29) Then he promptly promoted these men in the province of Babylon.

THE DEN OF LIONS

Similarly in Daniel Chapter 6, King Darius had a number of administrators in his kingdom who were jealous of young Daniel who had found favor in the sight of the king. Through trickery on their part they managed to persuade the king to pass an edict that prevented anybody from praying to any god or man except Darius himself. Daniel was thrown into the den of lions resulting in another profound deliverance on the part of God. The king then had those who falsely accused Daniel thrown into the lions along with their families. Then he also issued a decree that stated:

> *"I issue a decree that in every part of my kingdom people must fear and reverence the God of Daniel. For He is the living God and He endures forever; His kingdom will not be destroyed, His dominion will never end."* (Daniel 6:26)

In these case studies involving Shadrach, Meshach, Abednego and Daniel, their respective experiences of the fiery furnace and the den of lions can similarly represent for us today what may come against us as the people of God. The spirit of the world will challenge us with whatever is unfair and whatever is out of alignment; prejudices that will rise up against us, jealousies that occur, every type of human and demonic based fear, betrayal, broken loyalties and broken promises. They will separate us from what is normally safe and familiar, and expose us to the violation of the world. In other words, our faith is *on the line*. It either affirms or denies the authenticity of our belief systems and validates for us the truth of Psalm 31:15 — *"My times are in Your hands; deliver me from my enemies."*

FROM ACCUSATION TO VINDICATION

Isaiah 54:16–17 reminds us of God's ultimate authority in whatever circumstances we experience as His people. Verse 17 clearly states: *"...no weapon forged against you will prevail, and you will refute every tongue that accuses you. This is the heritage of the servants of the Lord, and this is their vindication from Me..."*

As we learn to minister in the power of the opposite spirit, we will find, just as these men did when faced with formidable odds, that the places of confinement and horror and probable death can instead become:

A place of refining;

A place of repositioning;

A place of recalibration;

A place of redefining and reaffirming our identity in the Lord;

A place where temptation is addressed and overcome;

A place where betrayal is crucified;

A place where we hide God's words and promises in our hearts for a season that is yet to come;

A place where unlikely rescue takes place on God's terms so that we can take no glory for ourselves;

A place where God imparts authority in our anointing once the fleshiness has been removed;

A place where obedience to God's Word establishes His fear in our lives as well as an undeniable reassurance that He is our 'plumb line' of reference.

This, in turn, establishes and releases:

    Integrity

    Authority

    Purity

    Strategy

    Insight

    Tenacity

    Faithfulness

    Loyalty

    Longevity

It is when we have this testimony of the fear of the Lord at work in our lives and as we choose to work in the power of the opposite spirit that, for those who are hidden with Christ in God (Colossians 3:3), the Lord releases:

    His healing;

    His deliverance;

    His forgiveness;

    His identity in us;

    His destiny for us;

    His direction for what lies ahead;

    His correction whenever necessary;

    His reviving power in our midst;

    His transformation in our lives and in society;

    His protection over and around us at all times;

    His covenantal promises for us.

This is important because as we learn how to minister in the power of the opposite spirit, this releases:

    The mind of Christ within us;

    The identification of Christ within us;

Our access to an understanding of how to appropriate the 'heavenly cycle of prayer' when it comes to releasing the fear of God in our society; (as explained in Chapter 6)

An understanding of Jesus being our intercessor;

Awareness that His armor does protect us in season and out of season;

An increasing recognition of the power of the cross at work in our lives;

A preparation for His ongoing strategy for revival and breakthrough in and through us.

JOSEPH — FROM PRISONER TO PRIME MINISTER

There are several examples in Scripture of others who went through similar times of testing and challenge. Consider Joseph (Genesis 37 to 47) who went through a process of being deserted, disowned and betrayed both by his brothers but also by those in prison, as well as being tempted by the wife of one of Pharaoh's officials. As he held to the fear of the Lord in his life, God was able to promote him to the position of prime minister at one of the most serious moments of history at that time. We find in the context of Genesis 42:18, that Joseph eventually earns the trust of his brothers when he states that he fears God.

> The chief sin of man is that we have no fear of God.

Fearing God, therefore, saves us from falling into the lure of our own sinful nature, but also of others who may tempt us to do so. Paul teaches that no one is righteous (Romans 3:9–20) and in this context the implication of verse 18 is serious: **The chief sin of man is that we have no fear of God.** Pharaoh brought disaster upon his nation since he did not fear God (Exodus 9:29–30).

Exodus 18:21 is a template for many leaders who are developing strong leadership. These need to be people who are *"men who fear God...who hate dishonest gain."* In other words, these are people who will not take bribes either financially or Scripturally! There can be no diluting and changing of what God says into something that man can change for his own purpose and personal gain. When we permit this, sound doctrine and Biblical integrity are being jeopardized (1 Timothy 4:16).

Whether our experience is like that of being in a pit, a fiery furnace, or a den — learning to minister in the power of the opposite spirit actually releases the power of God to work in our lives. This is what I experienced that day in the airport, when a man who was so obviously angry at me, changed in his demeanour and attitude within a matter of seconds as soon as I asked for his forgiveness. At the Lord's prompting, I responded to him in the opposite spirit, even though it was not in my initial human thinking!

PAUL AND THE POWER OF MINISTERING IN THE OPPOSITE SPIRIT

In Romans 12:14–21 we read these amazing words:

> "Bless those who persecute you; bless and do not curse. Rejoice with those who rejoice; mourn with those who mourn. Live in harmony with one another. Do not be proud, but be willing to associate with people of low position. Do not be conceited. Do not repay anyone evil for evil. Be careful to do what is right in the eyes of everybody. If it is possible, as far as it depends on you, live at peace with everyone. Do not take revenge, my friends, but leave room for God's wrath, for it is written: "It is Mine to avenge; I will repay," says the Lord. On the contrary: "If your enemy is hungry, feed him; if he is thirsty, give him drink. In doing this, you will heap burning coals on his head." Do not be overcome by evil, but overcome evil with good."

This is a powerful passage of Scripture. In effect, it is the strategy God gives through Paul to the emerging church, instructing them how to address both spiritual and physical issues in all aspects of life. Similarly, in 1 Corinthians 4:11–13 Paul states:

> "To this very hour we go hungry and thirsty, we are in rags, we are brutally treated, we are homeless. We work hard with our own hands.

When we are cursed, we bless; when we are persecuted, we endure it;
when we are slandered, we answer kindly. Up to this moment we have
become the scum of the earth, the refuse of the world."

Then, if we read Paul's account of his hardships in 2 Corinthians 6:3–
10, we read his explanation of how the ministry of God's people will not
be discredited. In life we may experience troubles, hardships, distresses,
beatings, imprisonments and riots, hard work, sleepless nights, or hunger.
However, he explains that it is through purity, understanding, patience
and kindness, truthful speech in the power of God, using the weapons of
righteousness, whether in glory or dishonor, bad or good reports, known
or unknown, dying, that the people of God that will live on.

In reality, Paul is explaining the 'secret' of navigating the most challenging
moments of life (just as did Shadrach, Meshach, and Abednego, Daniel
and Joseph), and yet still overcoming in a manner that releases the full
measure of God's integrity and extends the Kingdom of God.

PICKING UP THE TOWEL — NOT THROWING IN THE TOWEL

In John 13, Jesus Himself models the power of this expression of the
kingdom of God. John 13:1 states: *"....having loved His own who were*
in the world, He now showed them the full extent of His love." This account
of Jesus and His disciples is well known. When He came to Simon Peter
and washed his feet, initially Peter resisted what Jesus was about to do.
But here Jesus is demonstrating the power of servanthood as expressed in
the kingdom of God. This was both the 'suffering servant' and the King
of Kings simultaneously expressing the heart and love (Hebrew: *chesed*;
Greek: *agape*) of God. The modelling of the power of the kingdom of God
was being revealed through this simple, yet profound act.

Jesus completed this act of humble service in these words of John 13:14–
15 — *"Now that I, your Lord and Teacher, have washed your feet, you also*
should wash one another's feet. I have set you an example that you should do as
I have done for you." It was this depth of love that lay behind His teaching
of the Beatitudes in Matthew 5:1–12, followed by His instructions in
verses 38–41:

> *"You have heard that it was said, "Eye for eye, and tooth for tooth." But I tell you, "Do not resist an evil person. If someone strikes you on the right cheek, turn to him the other also. And if someone wants to sue you and take your tunic, let him have your cloak as well. If someone forces you to go one mile, go with him two miles…"*

When we work in the fear of the Lord we learn how to minister in the power of the opposite spirit.

PAUL AND THE SNAKE

In Acts 28 we are given the account of Paul following the shipwreck that occurred on the island of Malta. The islanders gave both the soldiers and the prisoners a warm welcome following their ordeal in the storm. But note that in verse 3 we are told that Paul gathers brushwood and places it on the fire. This is the act of a leader who is also a servant. Although he is still a prisoner, he has been given immense favor due to his leadership on the ship throughout the storm that had just occurred. Now as he places fuel on the fire, a viper attracted by the heat places itself on his hand.

The islanders know this is a poisonous snake. However, verse 5 tells us that Paul simply shook the snake off into the fire. When we work in the fear of the Lord we learn how to minister in the power of the opposite spirit. Irrespective of what is sent our way and no matter what snakes may appear with their various forms of venom — whether lies, fear, misrepresentation, or anything that the world sends us, this can all simply be 'shaken off' if we do not accept the toxin! This is the power of working in the opposite spirit.

RESULTS OF WORKING IN THE OPPOSITE SPIRIT

Learning this essential principle of the fear of the Lord in our lives reaps many benefits:

It disempowers the enemy's control and right of entrance, which feeds on pride, status, entitlement and self–determination.

It disengages the right of the enemy to have his foothold in our lives, our families, our churches, our businesses or in whatever environment we find ourselves.

It means demonstrating the power of the kingdom of God in a practical and obedient manner, thus dismantling and disengaging the enemy's accusation.

It releases seasoned and mature leaders to get behind the new leaders affirming and modelling for them. Peter and John came down from Jerusalem and stood behind Philip who had been ministering in Samaria. Philip was a new leader but these more mature believers did not engage in jealousy or competiveness.

It leads to celebration of each other's gift sets.

It enables others to grow and excel.

It makes us sensitive to a higher authority. In Deuteronomy 1:32–33 the context is that God does not want His people to rebel but to trust in Him *"who went ahead of you on your journey, in fire by night and a cloud by day, to search out places for you to camp and to show you the way you should go."* It is the fear of the Lord in us that enables us to trust Him in the unknown that lies ahead of us.

It is the fear of the Lord ministering in the power of the opposite spirit that dismantles, disengages and defeats the opposition of the enemy that we will meet en route.

It leads to an understanding of Isaiah 49:2 which states: *"He made my mouth like a sharp sword, in the shadow of His hand He hid me; He made me into a polished arrow and concealed me in his quiver."* This means that in our life and work with the Lord, there will be times when we will be out in the front feeling exposed and vulnerable to whatever we may be facing. Yet at the same time we recognize that *"...He who began a good work in you* [us] *will carry it on to completion until the day of Christ Jesus."* (Philippians 1:6)

At the same time, there will be occasions we need to be hidden with Christ in God (Colossians 3:3) and be placed back in His quiver (Isaiah 49:2) — back in His place of protection and nurturing. It is so important that all of us in ministry in this day and age have our identity based on who we are in Christ, and not in what we do, or in our ministries, or in the work of our hands.

It means picking up the towel (John 13:1–5) and at times the kindling sticks (Acts 28:2–3), which become the fuel that ignites and sustains the fire of the Lord in our midst. This in itself is essential for authentic leadership activating what is on the mind and heart of the Lord.

It disentangles and removes the right of the snake to attach itself to us and we learn to 'shake it off'.

It releases the power, testimony, integrity and authenticity of the living God in a day and age when things are looking dark and uncertain.

As modelled by Jesus and Paul, it opens the hearts and eyes of our communities and cities to the Lord.

It is modelling and authenticating what servant leadership is all about.

THE POWER OF TURNING THE OTHER CHEEK

The entire Sermon on the Mount is in fact Jesus teaching us to apply the principles of the kingdom of God while we live here on earth. It is teaching us about the character of God, and what the commandments and the Law really mean for us today — learning how to live under the rule and reign of the kingdom of God and not under the limitations of the ruling systems of this world. Putting it simply, it is all about living in the power of the opposite spirit.

We have examined a number of these principles above, but within the context of the Sermon on the Mount, let us return to this one verse of scripture that is so often subject to misinterpretation. Matthew 5:39 states: *"But I tell you, Do not resist an evil person. If someone strikes you on the right cheek, turn to him the other also."* Rather than reacting and submitting to the fleshy ways in which the spirit of the world so often operates, we are to take the higher road and to apply the principles of the kingdom of God in our various relationships and circumstances.

To turn one's cheek simply means going beyond our normal way of doing things in order to right any wrong we may have done, or correctly to respond to the wrongs others have done to us. It is our refusing the enemy to have right of entry into whatever circumstance we may be encountering, thereby giving him a foothold. It is learning to see the other person through the eyes of the Lord and to seek the Lord's counsel for that person, even if they may be appearing to do us harm or wrong. It is about our willingness to do any necessary self–examination before the Lord to ensure that there is no sin or reaction within us against that person or whatever system it is that we might be encountering that might cause us to react.

After all, 1 John 4:19–21 reminds us of these very challenging words:

> *"We love because He first loved us. If anyone says, 'I love God,' yet hates his brother, he is a liar. For anyone who does not love his brother, whom he has seen, cannot love God, whom he has not seen. And He has given us this command: Whoever loves God must also love his brother."*

Romans 12:20, which is quoting Proverbs 25:21–22 says: *"…If your enemy is hungry, feed him; if he is thirsty, give him something to drink. In doing this, you will heap burning coals on his head."* Proverbs 25:22 adds in these words: *"…and the Lord will reward you."*

Here we see the benefits of learning how to pray and minister in the power of the opposite spirit. We are actually releasing the jurisdiction, the direction and the empowering of the kingdom of God into the entire situation when we turn the other cheek. This is not about being a pacifist or a wimp! It is about making restitution and reconciliation if, and when, necessary. Even more so, it is about releasing the counsel of God into the entire situation so that our earthly relationship with others comes under the jurisdiction of the kingdom of God. This is the principle that lies behind all of the teaching of Jesus found in the Sermon on the Mount.

Ministering in the power of the opposite spirit through turning the other cheek is not about allowing

> Praying for a release of the fear of the Lord is perhaps one of the most powerful weapons that we can appropriate from God's arsenal.

people to abuse us, but instead understanding the power of the Cross in the midst of the situation. It is knowing that if that power overcame death, then it can also overcome every single situation that we encounter while on the planet earth. It is about receiving His counsel and direction in whatever confronts us! He wants us to stand in His council to hear and receive and speak His word, otherwise we become subject to lies. This is what is implied in Jeremiah 23:18–22.

How then, do we apply all that we have seen so far in a practical way of learning how to pray for the release of the fear of the Lord in our churches, our businesses, our families, our cities and our nations? Praying for a release of the fear of the Lord is perhaps one of the most powerful weapons that we can appropriate from God's arsenal that can even demolish strongholds and arguments that establish themselves against the knowledge of God in our communities. If, what Paul says in 2 Corinthians 10:5 is correct, then it is, in fact, possible to take captive these arguments and strongholds and thoughts — indeed the fear of man — and make them all obedient to Christ.

In a world so subject to compromise, lawlessness and entitlement, it is important that we learn how to pray for the Lord to release His fear in our midst.

CHAPTER 4

RELEASING THE FEAR OF THE
LORD IN OUR MIDST

On one occasion, Duncan Campbell referred to the 1949 — 1953 revival in the Hebrides in these words:

> *"In writing of the movement, I would like first to state what I mean by revival as witnessed in the Hebrides. I do not mean a time of religious entertainment, with crowds gathering to enjoy an evening of bright gospel singing; I do not mean sensational or spectacular advertising — in a God–sent revival you do not need to spend money on advertising. I do not mean high–pressure methods to get men to an inquiry room — in revival every service is an inquiry room: the road and hillside become sacred spots to many when the winds of God blow. Revival is a going of God among his people, and an awareness of God laying hold of the community. Here we see the difference between a successful campaign and revival; in the former we may see many brought to a saving knowledge of the truth, and the church or mission experience a time of quickening, but so far as the town or district is concerned no real change is visible; the world goes on its way and the dance and picture –shows are still crowded: **but in revival the fear of God lays hold upon the community** [emphasis mine], moving men and women, who until then had no concern for spiritual things, to seek after God.* [1]

> The fear of the Lord is all about understanding the character of God and how this can be applied in our lives.

So far in this study in the fear of the Lord, we have looked at the urgency of being prepared and being aware of the seriousness of the times in which we live. There is a call upon the body of Christ to be sober and alert and to know how to respond and not merely to react to the various concerns and fears that are now gripping the planet earth. We have compared the fear of man to the fear of the Lord. We have seen what it is the Lord hates and how the fear of man is a snare. We have examined examples of the fear of the Lord in Scripture. We have noted this requires us to have an awe and reverence for God, a willingness to resist evil without compromise and the need to be obedient to whatever the Lord calls us to do no matter how much our human flesh may want to resist. We have seen what it means to pray in the power of the opposite spirit and have noted numerous benefits and insights from doing so.

The fear of the Lord is all about understanding the character of God and how this can be applied in our lives and within the context of where we live and work. This is what Duncan Campbell was describing when the fear of the Lord gripped the Hebrides in response to the prayers of just a few people.

Over the years, our ministry has had the privilege of travelling to many different nations and cities, teaching and sharing the principles of authentic transformational revival. As we have studied historical records of revival in various nations, and examined contemporary templates, the same principles of prayer are always in place. One such principle that requires repetition is that we can only really pray for authentic revival to take place to the degree that we have the fear of the Lord in our own lives before we pray for it to be released into our communities. That is what authenticates the manner in which we pray and gives authority in both the spiritual and the physical realms.

CWMBRAN, WALES

On 10 April, 2013 a remarkable move of God took place in the Victory Church located in Cwmbran, Wales. In the seven months that followed, over 150,000 people visited this church from 42 nations. Hotels were booked up, petrol (gas) stations were overloaded with cars coming from all parts of the United Kingdom, and taxi drivers said more people wanted to go to this church than even the pub. Many people involved in drugs suddenly came to a knowledge of Christ bringing healing and breakthrough in their lives. Over 1600 decisions for Christ were recorded, which did not include the initial days of this outpouring.

We went to meet with those who were in leadership at that time in August 2014 and asked what they felt lay behind this powerful move of God. The leadership had been teaching the people how to seek God and determine what was on His heart. They began to incorporate a heart of prayer in the church as a whole, which became strategic for the manner in which they welcomed people into their fellowship. But what was particularly key was that God had convicted several of the people including some of the leadership of a religious attitude. Part of this involved an unhealthy attitude towards other churches in the area.

Two of the leaders shared with us that during this seven–month period, God gave them increasing discernment on what was important to Him and 'fast tracked them in 7 months with wisdom'. Right from that first evening on April 10, social media began to share the message that God was at work and, within a very short period of time, hundreds of people converged upon that fellowship almost on a daily basis. But what was key was the repentance in the hearts on the part of leaders who responded to pray in the manner that God required of them. As a result, God released His presence in their midst which was followed by several months of notable miracles and signs and wonders, with hundreds of lives being changed for eternity.

THE HEBRIDES — 1948–1953

In his sharing on the revival in the Hebrides, Duncan Campbell[2] made it very clear that, although he acted as one of the key catalysts, he did not bring revival to the Hebrides. God had begun to move in the community before he even arrived in response to the prayers of a few people. He cited two elderly sisters — one 84 and one 82 — who both were burdened with the appalling state of life in their community.

People in those days were known to be God–fearing and yet knew little about salvation. A religious culture had permeated the area for many years, and this included even the reading of Scripture! Yet there was no sense of personal responsibility for sin and no understanding of the need of repentance. As the two women were tenacious in prayer, God gave them a vision of what He intended to do, and they in turn talked to the minister of the parish and shared what God had placed on their hearts. Subsequently, the minister and his elders began to pray on a weekly basis along with these two elderly saints.

During one of those evening meetings, a young deacon in the church read from Psalm 24:

> *"Who may ascend the hill of the Lord? Who may stand in His holy place? He who has clean hands and a pure heart, who does not lift up his soul to an idol or swear by what is false. He will receive blessing from the Lord and vindication from God his Savior."* (Psalm 24:3–5)

God suddenly moved in their midst and all those who were present were gripped by the conviction that this need of holiness was essential for a revival of God's presence to be released in their midst. Each was convicted with the necessity of clean hands and a pure heart. From that time on, and for the next several years, the move of God affected life in the Hebridean communities in a profound manner. Whether it involved people in the local pubs, people in school, people working in the fields, people in their fishing boats, or young people attending a dance in the local parish hall, life became permeated with the holy presence of God. As Duncan Campbell put it:

> *"Revival began in an awareness of God. Revival began when the Holy Ghost began to grip men..."* [3]

It was this conviction of sin and sense of God's holiness in their midst, and the release of the fear of God that so changed life for the people of the Hebrides during those years of revival.

The holiness of God had so permeated the land that during the years that followed this revival, not one crime was reported for almost 20 years.[4] In both this historical example of revival in the Hebrides as well as the more recent move of God in Cwmbran, Wales, what was similar in both situations was the sense of God's holiness, the need for repentance, taking personal responsibility for sin and praying with tenacity as God gave insight and direction. These are tangible expressions of the fear of God at work initiated by the prayers of just a few people who had received God's vision and heart for His people. Even when a few catch the heartbeat of the Lord, it can literally affect an entire community well beyond the walls of the Church.

There needs to be a hunger on the part of those who are praying for whatever is on God's heart. Again, if we look at the promise in Psalm 25:14, the Lord will give us His counsel, He will confide into our hearts what is on His heart, to the degree we have His fear at work in our lives. That is His promise! This hunger must then lead to a personal sense of accountability and responsibility for ensuring that we go through the process at a personal level before we can pray at a corporate level with any authenticity.

Praying the fear of the Lord actually begins with a personal self–examination as to how desperate we are for a penetrating, permeating move of God in our society. We then need to consider whether we are deeply committed enough to pay the price for such a move of God to occur, followed by our willingness to steward His presence in our midst. There are at least seven simple but necessary components that throughout revival history have always been apparent in the lives of those whom God calls to stand in the gap on behalf of their communities and cities. Simply put, these seven factors are as follows:

> **1. Humility** — This is the expression of moving in the power of the opposite spirit of what presently influences or dominates any area. Again, it is the manner in which we pick up the towel of

service and ministry, rather than throwing in the towel and giving up. It is where we choose to have the character and posture of Jesus Himself in our lives, and ask the Lord to reveal to us what has to be addressed at a personal level. Just as that young deacon in the Hebrides did, we also need to consider the words of Psalm 24 asking God to give a self–revelation of any sin that needs to be addressed.

2. Holiness — Being set aside for the purposes of God and willing to see ourselves as God sees us and not allowing any foothold of sin (Ephesians 4:27) to remain with any justification or compromise.

3. Integrity — That there is no contradiction between what we say and what we do, and that our character reflects the character of Jesus himself.

4. Transparency — That no hidden agendas or motives can lie hidden and subtly manipulate the manner in which we pray.

5. Unity — That we can see ourselves as part of a "divine jigsaw puzzle" in which we see each other as a necessary part of who we are as the ingathered body of Christ. It is not purely about function, but more about a conviction that we need each other in order for God to fulfill His higher purposes.

6. Vertically informed prayer with horizontal accountability — As we will see in Chapter 6, when we refer to the 'Heavenly Cycle of Prayer', we are praying in a manner in which we hear what is on the Lord's heart and then are willing to steward and embrace and act on whatever He requires of us.

7. Divinely inspired and divinely timed spiritual warfare encounters — We keep watch and we wait until the fear of the Lord engages us and shows us what to do, when to do it, how to do it and with whom to do it. This is about understanding the strategy and the timing of the Lord in our midst.

Jehoshaphat learned that it was the Lord's battle he was engaged in — and not his own (2 Chronicles 20:15) — and as a result the Lord released amazing strategy resulting in a profound victory (2 Chronicles 20:22–30). Gideon learned a similar lesson in the Lord's timing and strategy that led to victory (Judges 7:22–24). Under the leadership of Moses, the people of God learned the importance of standing firm and not being afraid, since it was the Lord who was fighting for their deliverance (Exodus 14:13–14).

As we will now see, He is the God of breakthrough and provision for those who revere Him and who observe His commands and walk in His ways (Deuteronomy 8:6–18).

CHAPTER 5

PRAYING THE FEAR OF THE LORD — BENEFITS AND BREAKTHROUGHS

We have looked in depth at various principles that are essential in our understanding of the whole subject of the fear of the Lord. We have seen what the fear of the Lord involves Biblically. We have also looked at a number of examples in both the Old and the New Testaments in which the fear of the Lord established the authority and the mandate of the Lord for His people and all that had been entrusted into their care. We have looked at the issues concerning the fear of man and numerous ways in which this affects us in our day–to–day life. We have looked carefully at how to move under the authority of the Lord by learning how to work in the opposite spirit in this day and age. We have seen the importance of responding and not reacting.

Initially we looked at the wake–up call that God is giving to His church today, utilizing an historical example of what happened in Darwin, Australia. As we read the signs of the times carefully and prayerfully, we realize that we, the church, are on the cusp of something very profound. It is essential that we understand how to implement the fear of the Lord, not out of manipulation and 'soulish expectation', but out of obedience to what God has called us to do.

Now, we turn to see what the benefits and insights are that we gain when the fear of the Lord is released in our midst, starting at a personal level, and then extending into the areas for which God has given us responsibility and vision. A.W. Tozer summarized experiencing the fear of God in these words:

> *"The fear of God is...astonished reverence. I believe that the reverential fear of God mixed with love and fascination and astonishment and admiration and devotion is the most enjoyable state and the most satisfying emotion the human soul can know."* [1]

REVISITING SOME SCRIPTURES

In Psalm 33:8 we learn that the earth is to fear the Lord and the inhabitants of the world are to stand in awe of Him. In Acts 2:43 we learn that awe (fear of the Lord) came upon every soul and this was followed with signs and wonders undertaken by the leadership. Again, in Acts 9:31 the fear of the Lord fell upon an entire territory just as we have seen in many examples of historical revival and outpourings: "...*the church throughout Judea, Galilee and Samaria enjoyed a time of peace."* What is key here is that the church in the territory grew in numbers under the empowering of the Holy Spirit while at the same time living in the fear of the Lord.

A friend of our family has been a city co-ordinator of strategic prayer for many years. She recently sent me this personal testimony concerning the fear of the Lord:

> *"There were some things going on in the church where I was living but I did not want to give the word of the Lord since I had been chastised earlier for doing this. But on one occasion during a Sunday service the Lord's presence came upon me powerfully and three times I said I was not going to give this word — due to the fear of man from the earlier experience of being told to say nothing. The Spirit of the Lord fell on me so hard I thought I would die... I could hardly even breathe... so I submitted to the Lord, and under leadership protocol released the word in this congregation of about 500 people. I then collapsed in my chair. Everyone present was in awe... the fear of the Lord was so strong... I was a trembling mess. The man behind me who was a wonderful Christian touched my shoulder and said, 'That took courage... You really do not know what you said...' I wanted to get up and run and hide...but I could not.*

Several months later one of the board members came to me and said, 'Everything you said was true and it was due to your word that day that things at the top started to be dealt with and were revealed'... I knew that if I did not do what the Lord prompted me to do I would be in trouble with the Lord and enter into rebelliousness..."

This woman, a mature Christian and a leader of leaders, experienced the fear of the Lord in her life and had to overcome the fear of man in order for the work to be done in that area. On her part, it was an act of obedience while at the same time she allowed her word to be tested and tried to ensure that indeed it was from the Lord and not from her own human spirit. On a separate occasion with her family, she did not want to follow the Lord's instruction, but the presence of the Lord and the fear of the Lord came upon her with such heaviness that it was essential that she was obedient. The life of a family member had been in the balance and the Lord called her to respond in such ways that correct medical procedures were undertaken and the family member survived.

In Deuteronomy 6:10–13, we learn that fearing the Lord affects how we serve him. In verses 10–12 God reminds His people concerning their houses, their wells, their vineyards and olive groves, that He is the one who provides what they require. But they are not to forget Him since only He could remove their slavery. We therefore serve Him out of response and love and thanksgiving. Let's now look more closely at some of the 'benefits' that come from fearing the Lord in the manner He has requested:

1. Fearing the Lord qualifies how we love Him. Deuteronomy 10:12–15 reminds us that as we fear the Lord and walk in His ways and love Him then, we will serve Him with our whole being since everything in the heavens and on the earth belongs to Him anyway.

2. Fearing the Lord releases purity in our lives (with no hidden agendas). (Psalm 19:9)

3. Fearing the Lord releases a hatred of evil and pride and arrogance, and we then hate what the Lord hates. (Proverbs 8:13)

4. Fearing the Lord extends our life — certainly in terms of quality if not longevity. (Proverbs 10:27)

5. Fearing the Lord releases security and refuge and safety. (Proverbs 14:26–27)

6. Fearing the Lord releases wisdom and humility. (Proverbs 15:33)

7. Fearing the Lord enables us to avoid evil. (Proverbs 16:6)

8. Fearing the Lord releases His insight, His counsel, His power, and His knowledge and stops us from prematurely judging from what we see and hear. (Isaiah 11:2–4)

9. Fearing the Lord enables one to be blameless and upright and one who can maintain integrity irrespective of circumstances. (Job 2:3)

These are amazing benefits that the Lord releases and instils within His people and within a territory when *His* fear rests upon us in response to our prayers.

John Bevere concludes his book *The Fear of the Lord*[2] with a chapter on the blessings of holy fear. He cites several Scriptures that reveal just how profound life is for those who choose to live and walk in the fear of the Lord. For example, he points out they are assured of angelic protection (Psalm 34:7), and the promise that they will lack nothing (Psalm 34:9). Bevere adds that God's eyes will be upon those who fear Him (Psalm 33:18), promising them His security and protection (Proverbs 14:26–27). Amazing promises — amazing grace!

As mentioned in the early chapters of this book, there are hundreds of references to the fear of the Lord — each providing us with profound and practical insight as to how to live life in such a manner that releases His fullness in our lives. Is this not the promise of Jesus himself? *"The thief comes only to steal and kill and destroy; I have come that they may have life, and have it to the full."* (John 10:10)

As we obey the commandments of the living God and remain in His love, then the testimony of Jesus to His people is impacting: *"I have told you this so that My joy may be in you and that your joy may be complete. My command is this: Love each other as I have loved you. Greater love has no one than this, that he lay down his life for his friends."* (John 15:11–13) This is true for both the individual and for any corporate assembly, any business, any church, any territory, any city in which the people in that area have positioned themselves in the gap and asked for the fear of the Lord to come and rest in their midst.

MANCHESTER, KENTUCKY (THE CITY OF HOPE)

One of the most remarkable examples of contemporary community transformation that continues to affect life at all levels is found in Manchester, Kentucky. This is a rural community which, up until 2003, was faced with disproportionate levels of corruption, drugs, teenage suicide and a general sense of overall hopelessness. The Sentinel Group produced a DVD entitled *An Appalachian Dawn*,[3] which portrayed the graphic shift that took place in the life of that city as a result of hands–on prayer. I asked two of the leaders who were involved in that time of ministry to share in this book their testimony concerning the degree to which the fear of the Lord was involved in the profound change that took place:

> *"In 2003, as a handful of folks began to sincerely pray for the Lord's help, we knew the fear of the Lord was the beginning of wisdom. We desperately needed His wisdom if we were going to see change. What we had done for years did not work. We were frustrated, afraid, and negative. Our frustration caused us to begin to seek Him. The more we sought Him the more wisdom we gained, and the more we heard His instructions to us. Even before we saw any tangible results we sensed a stirring. We dared to begin to believe that* change *could occur.*
>
> *I remember we found Psalm 34:11 — 'Come listen... I will teach you the fear of the Lord.' A reverence, a greater respect for the Lord began to manifest in our lives. Knowing that the Lord was bigger and more powerful than drug dealers and corrupt politicians, we began to wait upon the Lord expecting Him to speak to us. That is when Pastor Ken*

Bolin had the dream of marching for the glory of God. Looking back on it later, we realized the fear of the Lord had gripped our hearts. God had rewarded the obedient and judged the disobedient."

Change continues to develop in Manchester and more recently they have undergone a process of staking the land and praying the canopy of the Lord over their community, which we will examine in Chapter 6. God continues to deepen His vision and His direction in their lives and even at times, when there has been a temporary setback in what progress had taken place, the Lord has showed them where the 'holes in the fence' have occurred, and how to repair them. The fear of the Lord is a continuum at all levels in our lives to the degree that we continually call upon the Lord for His awe and reverence to be within our lives, and for us to respond with obedience and to resist any subtle form of compromise to what His Word may require.

SOUTHLAND CHURCH, STEINBACH, MANITOBA

One of the most current templates of emerging transformational change is located in Steinbach, a rural area of Manitoba, Canada. Traditionally known as a Mennonite community, this church has grown immeasurably into a fellowship of several thousand people, which now hosts renewal weekends and is influencing leadership across various nations. It holds regular prayer meetings at times in excess of 1000 people. The senior pastor has indicated that what has brought the greatest amount of transformation in his life has been the fear of the Lord.

> The fear of the Lord enables us to bring a holy alignment of His purposes into every area of our lives.

Our own pastor has now begun to implement many of the principles God has shown this fellowship in Steinbach. When he received my query concerning the importance of the fear of the Lord in both Steinbach but also in the church–at–large, he was with the members of his 'church renewal mentoring group', which is associated with this church in Steinbach. Here are his comments:

> *"God really entered into our discussion and we got talking about the **fear of the Lord** and our absolute need as ministers to die to ourselves and surrender our will completely to the will of Christ. In fact we all took time to kneel in prayer and consecration at the foot of one of the crosses that was erected in our meeting room. It was a holy moment."*

As we have been seeing so far, having the fear of the Lord in our midst releases among other things His provision, His righteousness, His truth and His joy in our midst. This is due to the fact that the fear of the Lord enables us to bring a holy alignment of His purposes into every area of our lives. Whatever is out of order will very quickly be highlighted and we will choose to put things back in Godly order to the degree that the weightiness of the Lord rests in our midst. This was the experience of our friend cited above who was the city coordinator for intercession. The Amplified version[4] of Ecclesiastes 12:13 puts it this way:

> *"All has been heard; the end of the matter is: Fear God (revere and worship Him, knowing that He is) and keep His commandments, for this is the whole of man (the full, original purpose of his creation, the object of God's providence, the root of character, the foundation of all happiness, the adjustment to all inharmonious circumstances and conditions under the sun) and the whole duty of every man."*

BLESSINGS AND BENEFITS

For those who walk in the fear of the Lord (Psalm 128:1) the **blessings and benefits** are both extraordinary and unlimited.

In Psalm 23:5 we are told that God prepares a table right in front of our enemies. This is a divine promise assuring us of God's intervention on our behalf when we are faced with difficult moments that we encounter in our earthly life.

When we walk in the fear of the Lord we are given the assurance that the Lord enters into every arena and circumstance of life and walks through

> No matter our age or status in life, His word promises to bless those who fear the Lord.

those issues with us. He wants our hearts to desire His fear in order that all will go well for us — and our children. This is a generational promise. (Deuteronomy 5:29)

In Psalm 31:19 He promises His goodness in our lives for those who take refuge in His life. What an amazing promise! His life and His goodness is in us to the degree that we take refuge in Him. He becomes our help and shield in the process. (Psalm 115:11)

No matter our age or status in life, His word promises to bless those who fear the Lord. (Psalm 115:13) Indeed, this is a promise for everybody who is willing to walk in His ways. (Psalm 128:1) Above all, walking in the fear of the Lord assures us of clarity in any decision–making that may need to undertake. Jeremiah 32:39 states it this way: "*I will give them singleness of heart and action, so that they will always fear Me for their own good and the good of their children after them.*"

As we reflect on what we have seen above and in the early chapters of this book, the fear of the Lord assures us that He will confide in us (Psalm 25:14) — that He will provide for us (Psalm 111:5) — and that His mercy and compassion will be extended to those that fear Him generationally, in our lives, our families, our churches, our businesses, our cities and even our nations. (Luke 1:50) What an extraordinary promise — "*His mercy extends to those who fear Him, from generation to generation.*" To be blessed with the love and faithfulness of the Lord in this way actually goes beyond human comprehension.

This, of course, is what lies behind the gift of His son Jesus Christ (John 3:16). God longs to pour out His love in and through our lives in an ever–increasing measure. But those who call upon the fear of the Lord are the ones who more will readily identify and experience this depth of love. This happens when He has full access in their lives and His kingdom rule and reign is in their midst. This is why the Lord has compassion upon those who fear Him just as a father has compassion on his children (Psalm 103:13).

Therefore, to summarise, the fear of the Lord ....

> **Promises** protection from the missiles and battles of life and reminds us He is our rear guard. (Isaiah 52:12; 58:8)
>
> **Provides** us with His supernatural intervention and provision in our lives.
>
> **Reveals** His Godly parameters for us.
>
> **Discloses** what is on God's heart for us.
>
> **Eliminates** what is superfluous to Him — and therefore to us.
>
> **Provides direction** even when He appears to be 'silent'.
>
> **Removes ungodly toxins** — any form of consumerism and unhealthy and unwitting worship in our lives (of things, people, activities, hobbies).
>
> **Explains** how we are to pray the will of God into any given situation.
>
> **Separates fantasy** from truth and authenticates reality — so that we see things from God's point of view.

The question that we need to ask of ourselves is this: "How desperate are we for a penetrating, permeating move of God in our society"? If we are desperate to the point where we will say *yes* irrespective of circumstances, then will we pay the price? Will we then continue to steward His presence in our midst? This is the key challenge for many communities at this time.

THE AMAZING STORY OF CALI, COLOMBIA

In the original *Transformations* DVD[5] produced by the Sentinel Group, one of the cities cited was Cali, Colombia. Several people were catalysts for this amazing move of God that continues to this very day. Ruth Ruibal and her husband Julio were among these original catalysts. Ruth has said to us personally, *"The change continues in Cali, Colombia; the darkness brought by the drug cartel is gone, and the atmosphere is open to the Gospel —many are still coming to the Lord and churches are growing. To date we are still praying together in the stadium each year."* I asked Ruth this question: *"*Did you sense a fear of God during the move of God in Cali?" Here is her response:

> *"I see the importance of persecution today in a completely different way than most people. For us the move of God in Cali came during a time of great trial, persecution and threats, along with our beloved city that had been completely sold out to corruption under the drug lords. It was God's grace and mercy that actually worked out the first all–night prayer meeting — the coliseum had been rented by a ministry and the man who was to come was not able to do so. With the coliseum already rented, we decided to have a prayer meeting to see if the Lord just might have mercy on us and our lost city.*
>
> *His response to united prayer was most outstanding as one can see in the Transformations* [6] *video — the cartel fell, the previously very closed–to–the–Gospel city became open to the Gospel overnight — a truly miraculous change that brought thousands to the Lord... we needed to know what the Lord wanted, what His will was. We knew that if we did things in our own way or strength we could easily fall back into the darkness that the Lord was delivering us from. No one talked about the Fear of the Lord, but it was functioning among us. It is a carefulness to know the Lord's will and walk in His paths....*
>
> *The church in general...has lost much of the fear of God... we get caught up in emotionalism and forget what happens when we do things our own way — and like Nadab and Abihu, the fire that consumed the burnt offering when the presence of God came down and brought the people of Israel into real worship and prostrate on their faces, is the same fire that came out of the presence of God to consume these men who tried to worship in their own way."*

This, of course, is what the fear of the Lord is all about. As we saw in Chapter 1 it is a combination of awe, reverence, obedience and the desire to resist evil no matter how enticing it might be. At the same time it releases a fear in us if we go beyond the boundaries and the guidelines that God has prepared for those who love Him and walk in His fear. It is how we can live life today in the fullness the Lord has prepared for us.

> God is always inviting us to a different way of thinking.

In Luke chapter 3 when John the Baptist was preaching his sermon on repentance, his words convicted the hearts and minds of those who were present. The crowd, the tax collectors, and even the soldiers — these groups representing so many components of society at that time — all asked John the Baptist the same question, *"What should we do?"*

WHAT SHOULD WE DO?

These chapters have been an intensive journey for me personally as I have written these words and recounted the many times that the fear of the Lord has interrupted my life and circumstances. The busyness of life is often the worst competitor for the fear of the Lord in my life on a personal level.

However, it is my belief that it is time for the people of God to recover the fear of the Lord in the remaining time we have before the return of the bridegroom for His bride. My firm belief is that the Lord is at this moment preparing His bride, and as we read His Word in both an historical and prophetic context, I believe time is running out. Not unlike those who responded to the sermon of John the Baptist, we might well also ask a similar question: *"What **must** we do?"*

Recently we were talking with friends about the fear of the Lord and what God is calling us to do in this day and age. One of these friends, Sid, made this comment to us: *"God is always inviting us to a different way of thinking."* As my wife and I were talking about this afterwards with particular reference to the fear of the Lord, it was as if the Lord said: *"As you align your thoughts to the thoughts of God... He shows His perspective for each of us in every scenario and possibility... and brings us into His peace."*

This is a decision that we need to enter into for ourselves and then a choice that we make to pray this into our communities with integrity and purity and understanding: *"He will be the sure foundation for your times, a rich store of salvation and wisdom and knowledge; the fear of the Lord is the key to this treasure."* (Isaiah 33:6)

CHAPTER 6

ARISE, O LORD GOD, AND COME TO YOUR RESTING PLACE

Solomon's prayer of dedication in 2 Chronicles 6:12–42 comes right from his heart and is a direct request to the Lord to come to the temple that has been prepared for His presence. It is a prayer is one of deep intimacy in which the king states that whatever is contrary to the presence of the Lord will be addressed. As he concludes, he says these words:

> *"Now, my God, may Your eyes be open and Your ears attentive to the prayers offered in this place. Now arise, O Lord God, and come to your resting place, you and the ark of your might..."* (2 Chronicles 6:40–41).

What follows confirms that the Lord receives the prayer:

> *"When Solomon finished praying, fire came down from heaven and consumed the burnt offering and the sacrifices, and the glory of the Lord filled the temple."* (2 Chronicles 7:1)

His presence came into their midst. We see a similar request on the part of the Psalmist in Psalm 132:8. When the people of God ask the Lord to arise, and they seek His presence on His terms and with the necessary protocol in place, He will respond — though He reserves the right to determine when and in what manner. Note what the Lord says Himself in this regard:

> *"Because of the oppression of the weak and the groaning of the needy, I will now arise," says the Lord. "I will protect them from those who malign them."* (Psalm 12:5–6)

> And again in Isaiah 33:10 — *"Now will I arise", says the Lord. "Now will I be exalted; now will I be lifted up."*

While the presence of the Lord would fill His temple in the Old Testament days, this was also a precursor of what would come in the New Testament days. Paul puts it this way in 1 Corinthians 3:16–17 —

> *"Don't you know that you yourselves are God's temple and that God's spirit lives in you? If anyone destroys God's temple, God will destroy him; for God's temple is sacred, and you are that temple."*

Profound words! Our bodies become the temple of the Holy Spirit (1 Corinthians 6:19). Then we have these remarkable words from Paul in 2 Corinthians 6:16–17 —

> *"…For we are the temple of the living God. As God has said: 'I will live with them and walk among them, and I will be their God, and they will be My people.'"*

Because we are His 'temple', it is therefore both individual and corporate. When the fear of the Lord is prayed for by the people of God, and they ask Him to arise and to come into their midst, and align themselves with His protocol, then individuals and even entire communities are impacted by the power of His presence. It is a matter of aligning ourselves with His ways and His thoughts (Isaiah 55:8–9).

ALIGNING OUR THOUGHTS WITH THE THOUGHTS OF GOD

Romans 8 is a good encapsulation of the manner in which God wants us to be praying for whatever is on His heart. This is powerful — God has a purpose He wants to share with us here on earth. He sends the Holy Spirit to us to tell us what is on His heart and we begin interceding as the Holy Spirit brings us revelation. Then it is Jesus who becomes our advocate. He makes intercession on our behalf before the throne of God (Romans 8:26–39). This is totally amazing! We are God's advocates on earth, but

Jesus is our advocate who takes back to the throne of grace what is already on the Father's heart. We call this the '**Heavenly Cycle of Prayer**'.

Therefore, the three persons of the Godhead are continually functioning on our behalf. The Father sends the Holy Spirit. The Holy Spirit intercedes through us, telling us what is on the Father's heart. Jesus becomes our advocate and mediator taking the request to the Father who initiated the prayer in the first place! This is the assurance of Hebrews 11:1 —

> *"Now faith is being sure of what we hope for and certain of what we do not see."*

It is what we read in 1 John 5:14–15 —

> *"This is the confidence we have in approaching God; that if we ask anything according to His will, He hears us. And if we know that He hears us — whatever we ask — we know that we have what we asked of Him."*

We, therefore, are praying the prayer of the Godhead. This is the ongoing cycle of prayer that intercessors are responding to as under God's direction. As we pray in this manner, we are standing in that place of responsibility, responding to what is on the heart of God. This is how we begin to release the fear of the Lord in our midst just as those elderly women did in the Hebrides and just as more recently took place in Cwmbran, Wales.

ACCESSING OUR COMMUNITIES WITH TARGETED PRAYER

In our book *God's Design for Challenging Times*,[1] we outline what we refer to as the major access points for prayer in every community. We refer to the church, the legal arena, the political arena, the area of education, the area of industry, trade and commerce, the area of media, the medical arena, and finally even the area involving the armed forces.

While there are many other areas that could be included, we have found these to be the primary targets for informed and effective prayer. In each of these areas of life and work, informed intercessors and leaders should be continually asking the right questions in order to fight the right battles so that the presence of the Lord will be released in our midst.

ASK THE RIGHT QUESTIONS — FIGHT THE RIGHT BATTLES

An initial question is: **Why are people spiritually blind to the things of God in any given area?**

> When the fear of the Lord is released in our midst we gain deep understanding into these things that are on the heart of God.

Paul says in 2 Corinthians 4:4 — *"The god of this age has blinded the minds of unbelievers, so that they cannot see the light of the gospel of the glory of Christ, who is the image of God."* If our church, our community, our business or our city is not able to embrace the things of the Lord on His terms, the question is, why?

The worldview of Scripture in both the Old and New Testaments is that the spiritual realm has an immense cause–and–effect relationship with the physical realm. Principalities and powers do exist. There is ongoing activity in the heavenlies. What takes place here on earth is often a representation of what is going on in the spirit realm. Therefore, if we are unable to perceive this, there will be a mindset or a stronghold prohibiting us from understanding this important principle (2 Corinthians 4:4). This question enables us to ask why things are the way they are, in order to be praying with insight and understanding. This is why we need to understand the activity of the Godhead that involves us in the heavenly cycle of prayer.

Another question to ask is: **In what manner is the enemy at work in our various neighborhoods and communities?** Whether it is in our churches, businesses, or in our cities — leadership and intercessors need to have an understanding from God's point of view, as to what is on His heart regarding what is affecting the people on the land. Our understanding and insight is finite, while God's understanding and insight is infinite. He is the Alpha and the Omega, the Beginning and the End. Therefore He knows what will have taken place in any given area that continues to have consequences upon the people who live and work in that area both in the years past, the years present, and the years yet to come. When the fear of the Lord is released in our midst we gain deep understanding into these things that are on the heart of God.

A further question to ask is: **What is the strategy and timing concerning what we are to do under God's direction?** If we are his stewards of the land, then it is our responsibility to address issues that affect the ebb and flow of life; especially if what is taking place is contrary to God's purposes. Scripture indicates it is our responsibility to bind and to loose (Matthew 16:19), and it is our responsibility to guard and keep and occupy in order to avoid unnecessary attrition. (Matthew 12:43–45) When the fear of the Lord is prayed into and over a city, God reveals, informs, gives insight, and gives instruction on what needs to be done.

As we have seen over the years, when properly undertaken in each of the access points referred to above, a tangible evidence of the presence of God can enter into these access points if the right people are praying in the way God has instructed them. There is nothing manipulative whatsoever about this type of prayer — it is a form of stewardship responsibility on our part as we respond to what is on God's heart. It is in fact, appropriating what the power of the Cross is all about.

We start with ourselves.

We address any areas of sin that the Lord reveals, both past and present, and repent before Him for the sin, asking His forgiveness. Then we extend this into a corporate prayer. This is what lay behind Solomon's Prayer in 2 Chronicles 6.

For us today, it is about appropriating the grace of Christ that is made available through the atoning work of Christ on the Cross. It is this that can break the bondages and remove the strongholds that blind people from the knowledge of the glory of the gospel of Christ. This is true both individually and corporately. It does not mean that people automatically come to Christ — but, as we have seen in countless examples in historical and contemporary revivals, the power of God enters into these arenas of life and activity, and pierces the hearts of unbelievers and opens their eyes to the reality of the power of the message of salvation.

Any footholds the enemy has accessed are then revealed and addressed since the sin that was the foundation for such footholds has now been identified, repented of, and removed. Then the actual healing of the land (2 Chronicles 7:14) can be appropriated in a manner that releases the heart and purpose and destiny of the Lord in any given area. That is the power of the cross at work.

LAND — THE MEETING PLACE BETWEEN GOD AND MAN!

For over 30 years we have been teaching the subject of 'land' in many parts of the world. In one of our earlier books, *Releasing Heaven on Earth,*[2] we provide much Biblical teaching and insight and practice on how to see the healing of the land occur as under God's direction. To summarize this whole area of teaching, we would state that:

The land contains the product of blessing and curse from previous years and generations.

This becomes a 'feeding trough' for whatever takes place on that area (whether a church, a business, a city, a nation etc.) that affects both present and future generations.

> Land becomes a non–negotiable component in our praying for the fear of the Lord to be released into our communities.

Until the present–day stewards address these issues; then the issues from the past still have a spiritual cause–and–effect. This allows a spiritual malaise to linger in that place, blinding the minds of the people from the gospel of Christ (2 Corinthians 4:4).

Until this malaise is addressed, the productivity and fruitfulness God would want for that area is subject to robbery, exploitation, usury and whatever may be opposite to God's purpose for that place. This is what minimizes the ability of the people of God in appropriating and releasing His vision for that area with authority and authenticity. In particular, we have often seen this as a major factor that impedes effective and sustainable church planting.

The land represents God's 'opinion' of things! The word 'land' is referred to over 1700 times in Scripture, and we need to bear in mind that it is the meeting place between God and man.

Land becomes a non–negotiable component in our praying for the fear of the Lord to be released into our communities and cities. Whatever takes place upon land is of consequence to God! Joel 2:18 reminds us that God is jealous for His land. We are reminded in Isaiah 24:5–6 that the earth is defiled when its people have disobeyed the laws of God. As a result, a curse consumes the earth and the people must bear the consequences as well as undertake the remedy. Jeremiah understood this principle: *"O Land, land, land, hear the word of the Lord!"* (Jeremiah 22:29)

Consequently, on many occasions we have found that a blindness towards God and an inability of perceiving His existence exists in such areas. In essence, it is as if a 'shroud' covers the area influencing the people and their life and work — and even their worship. This remains until the issues on the land are correctly addressed. Isaiah 25:6–12 reveals the desire of the Lord to remove such a shroud that affects His people in order that the fullness of His purpose can be made known to them. We will now see how this can actually be undertaken under God's direction as we begin to pray the fear of the Lord into our communities.

SHROUD VS. CANOPY — IT'S OUR CHOICE!

A 'shroud' can cover any size of community or city or even a territory and can, in turn, blind their eyes from understanding and perceiving the purposes of God in their midst. We will now look at some of the ways that God has taught us to pray for the release of His fear over an area, and how he replaces a shroud with his canopy.

It is so important that those who are involved in this type of prayer posture are people themselves who are willing to go through the same process that they want to have released in their communities. We must always bear in mind however, that any strategy of implementation will vary from one area to another, depending on the counsel and direction of the Lord. For the purpose of this book, we are offering examples of prayer strategies that have proven to be highly effective in several case studies.

In Isaiah 4:5–6 we read these words:

> "*Then the Lord will create over all of Mount Zion and over those who assembled there a cloud of smoke by day and a glow of flaming fire by night; over all the glory will be a canopy. It will be a shelter and shade from the heat of the day, and a refuge and hiding place from the storm and rain.*"

In this passage Isaiah is using the imagery of the Exodus (Exodus 13:21–22 to remind Israel to see her entire history as one that is under the Lord as a "canopy". There is both a sense of deep intimacy as well as divine love and protection in using such a descriptive word. It is God's holy desire to have His people living and working under His canopy.

Then in Isaiah 40:21–23 —

> "….*Have you not understood since the earth was founded? He sits enthroned above the circle of the earth, and its people are like grasshoppers. He stretches out the heavens like a canopy, and spreads them out like a tent to live in.*"

In Psalm 104:2 the Psalmist offers this image of the Lord:

> "*He wraps himself in light as with a garment; He stretches out the heavens like a tent…*"

There is amazing imagery and intent on the part of the Lord in verses such as these. We sense that the Lord wants to 'over–arch' His people and provide protection and cover for them. Yet, where the enemy of God's people has been given the right of a foothold, one that may exist on the land even generationally, this creates a vulnerability in that area. People can at times sense a tangible spiritual pressure in such places, which is due to the spiritual issues at work there. In basic spiritual warfare terms, this is due to the fact that the enemy has had access to the people and systems of life there, and has blinded them from the intent and love of the Lord.

Through informed and properly disciplined "hands on" acts of prayer and ministry (that include repentance and even restitution when necessary) God can change the spiritual climate in any area. This will affect the systems of life. Any 'shroud' that affects an area is addressed under the direction of the Lord. Then prophetically, we can be praying the canopy of the Lord to be positioned over that place and ask the Lord to release the destiny, fullness and authority of His presence in the midst of the people.

On one occasion we were asked to go and visit a large ministry centre in the United Kingdom. Various issues had taken place over a period of time, and we had arrived in order to conduct a seminar on intercession. Along with various members of the leadership, we applied the teaching as an actual template of prayer in which issues were addressed that would have given the enemy access to that area. This, in turn, would have affected the people who would minister and work there, as well as those entering the property. In effect, we were removing the shroud and erecting the canopy of the Lord.

Together we walked through the buildings and around the land, sharing what insights and Scriptures that God was impressing upon as we did this. We used salt, water and oil, prophetic agents of cleansing and anointing, in both the interior and the exterior of the buildings. The words of Scripture unique to this specific time of ministry, which the Lord brought to mind collectively during this process, were written on wooden stakes (Isaiah 54:2–3; Isaiah 33:20–22). These, in turn, were then planted deeply into the ground at specific entry and exit points of the land, as well as along the boundary lines of the land itself. We were declaring God's intent and destiny for this land and ministry.

Finally, we corporately prayed while standing at the four corners of the property at a mutually agreed time, since we were then out of sight of each other due to the size of the property.

One of the co-ordinators sent a testimony concerning the change that took place in the days and weeks that followed.

> *"For me, it was a 'seminal moment' along with the teaching on intercession. The spiritual atmosphere certainly changed for the better. We had visitors coming in who hadn't been here for maybe a couple of years, who asked us "What has happened? This place is very different!" As leaders there was a freedom we hadn't had... Not to say that we don't have to work on keeping it! Guard, occupy and keep! "*

Similar to this testimony from the United Kingdom, we were asked to work with a leadership team in Canada who direct a ministry that is involved in healing and transformation. They had recently been given ownership of five acres of property, which would become their new place of operation. Here is the testimony from the Director following a "hands on" time of ministry asking for the fear of the Lord to be released on their land.

> *"It began as a dreary, damp and overcast day. Using salt and water and anointing oil we began cleansing and anointing the home moving to the outside of the building. As a team, we prepared stakes with Scriptures that reflected our purpose, and words God had given to us. We then staked the four corners of the property. The team began to feel much lighter (in spirit) and excitement increased as we proceeded. With the team in place at each corner of the property, we prayed and lifted the shroud off the land and building, and then placed the 'canopy of God' over the land. Just as this happened, the clouds cleared away, the birds sang loudly and the sun shone upon us and the land. It was a beautiful experience and we all knew something significant had happened. I prayed that the Lord would allow His creation to flourish in this place....during the next week we saw a cow moose and calf as well as six deer resting on the land. We had not seen them here before. In addition, ministry to individuals on this land has brought revelation and healing in greater ways than we have experienced previously...*

We have had numerous testimonies such as this over many years in which an observable, experiential shift has taken place after this type of prayer ministry was applied in a given area. While it is not necessarily "automatic", if such prayer is stewarded correctly there can well be a substantial change in the systems of life that occur in such areas in the months and years that follow. We simply follow the outline for prayer that we established earlier in this chapter — addressing sins and repentance, breaking bondages, addressing any demonic activity, praying for God's healing to be released upon that area (the land and the people) which is His promise in 2 Chronicles 7:14 and then making any necessary restitution as God requires. This becomes a model that is totally flexible and adaptable to any type of situation as under the direction and anointing of the Lord.

LAND CAN ACTUALLY BE HEALED AND CHANGED

We have prayed for people over many years believing that healing and deliverance were just a normal part of ministry (Luke 9:11). But we had never really taken seriously what healing of the land meant — and certainly not in such a literal way, until the Lord soundly challenged us on this subject during a particular time in pastoral ministry. Many years have passed and we have literally seen hundreds of templates of shift and change as promised in Leviticus 26:3–10 in which the fear of the Lord came upon the people in an area which substantially changed the way they lived and worked.

We have seen land healed, the ecology return in an area, economics shift in an area and levels of security shift when crime diminishes and societal responsibility increases. We have seen amazing shifts in conversion growth, and we have seen the Lord take areas that were impoverished and bless them and shift them and change them with a purpose and distinctiveness that reflects what we read in Leviticus 26:11–13 —

> *"I will put My dwelling place among you, and I will not abhor you. I will walk among you and be your God, and you will be My people. I am the Lord your God, who brought you out of Egypt so that you would no longer be slaves to the Egyptians; I broke the bars of your yoke and enabled you to walk with **heads held high**."* (emphasis mine)

We have seen integrity and purpose and distinctiveness return to the lives of people, churches, businesses, communities and areas where people have implemented such acts of ministry in a way that demonstrates the fullness of the kingdom of God. Indeed, it is in effect a repositioning of the "canopy" — the protection, direction, provision and even the correction of the Lord in any given area.

At times people question why this is not seen in the New Testament. In reality the teaching in the New Testament is based on fulfilling and appropriating the teaching of the Old Testament. Jesus is clear that He did not come to abolish the Law or the Prophets but to fulfill them and affirm this would be accomplished (Matthew 5:17–18). Prayer walks, for example, are a very regular way of life for many people in several parts of the world today. But I remember well when these were regarded as something totally new and unheard of and yet, the Old Testament is replete with people walking on the land, inspecting the territory and becoming familiar with their terrain in order to bring in the purpose of God under His direction.

Joshua 6, concerning the battle of Jericho, gives clear insight into the strategy of God concerning the principles of walking on the land. In the New Testament, Paul also modelled this in Acts 17:16–23 when he walked around Athens gaining an understanding that lay behind the mindset that affected the thinking of the people before he gave his famous exhortation in the meeting of the Areopagus.

The Salvation Army understood the importance of marches and walking the territory ever since its founding by William Booth in 1865. Years later, Graham Kendrick would institute praise marches called "March for Jesus". This revolutionized the way people understood their territory in so many parts of the world. Countless reports of shifts and changes in cities around the world began to pour in to headquarters in many nations.

Centuries ago the Anglican church understood the importance of "beating the bounds" in which the parish priest and the elders would regularly walk the entire circumference of their parish boundaries at least on an annual basis, sprinkling water and salt upon the land as they walked, and anointing certain points of the parish boundaries with oil. They would address any work of the enemy that had taken place there in the days that preceded this act of ministry. The leadership was asking for the fullness and the power and the glory of the Lord to meet the people of that area within their parish boundaries in the following days. Countless reports would take place in which people would be simply walking along the road and suddenly were confronted with the glory and the presence of the Lord, and then fall flat on the ground repenting before the Lord and asking Him to do business with them. The fear of the Lord had come upon the area.

In undertaking such acts of ministry, these should always be done under the instruction and direction of the Lord. Otherwise even ministry such as this can become mechanical and lifeless. When staking the land we are in fact using the stakes in a prophetic manner as we ask God to remove any mindset or stronghold that has had the right of access in that territory minimizing or negating whatever He wants to do with His people there. Our working definition of a stronghold is:

> "A sphere of influence upon and within our lives, families, churches, communities, cities and even nations that feeds upon sin (both individual and corporate, personal and inherited) that gives spiritual and geographical leverage to the enemy of God's people, thus blinding them to the truth of seeing things from God's perspective (2 Corinthians 4:4; 10:4–5)." [3]

Such strongholds readily exist in any of the access points that we referred to earlier. This is why at times it is hard for the Church to advance in an area. There can be corruption within the political and even legal systems. This is why the business arena may find it challenging to enter into authentic marketplace ministry.

However, when existing strongholds in such access points are removed, the fullness and purpose and direction of the Lord can be released into those areas and stewarded by those whom God has placed in those specific areas. When each person, church, business and organization seeks God's purpose in their respective areas of responsibility, then collectively individual breakthroughs can become a corporate breakthrough. In so doing, spiritual strongholds that have fed upon individual and corporate

> When the canopy of the Lord envelops any area, there is a distinct sense of God's custodianship!

sin, perhaps even generationally, can then be removed and replaced with a new sense of God's purpose and direction and destiny upon that area.

On one occasion we had the privilege to work with leaders in the business community of a city that owned and operated a commercial roofing company. After a time of prayer and cleansing their land, and also staking of the land with proper prayer protocol, significant shifts began to take place for these people. To this day, they continue the process of stewarding what God has entrusted to them and they continue to have breakthroughs in their business, which is truly a kingdom business. Here is their testimony as they sought the fear of the Lord in their midst and in their company:

> *"Prayer is the basis of who we are. Intimacy with Jesus has encouraged us to have a greater fear/respect for Jesus. As our intercessory prayer team prays for us the Holy Spirit flows through our family and our business and we witness Jesus working and this has given us a reverence, respect and fear that we could not have made possible on our own."*

Even during a time of recession, their business continued to grow. When the canopy of the Lord envelops any area, there is a distinct sense of God's custodianship! Indeed, as unholy strongholds are removed, it is the stronghold of the Lord that instead takes up residence on God's terms (Psalm 27:1).

PUTTING IT ALL TOGETHER

We have now looked at the Biblical background of what a shroud involves, and why strongholds may exist wherever people live, work, and worship upon the land. We understand the significance of the canopy of the Lord, as well as the use of stakes as a prophetic act. We now also need to look at the actual raising of the canopy, as and when the Lord directs.

Once the research and the practical steps as outlined above have been implemented, then those who have been meeting regularly, and waiting on the Lord, are ready to undertake whatever He has called His people to do. These are the ones standing in the gap. Now we are ready to implement the raising of the canopy as a prophetic act on behalf of the community.

Generally we walk the boundaries of the entire area over a period of time. This may be hours depending on the size of the project, or this may be days. We are not looking for a band–aid solution! Once we have gone through the process of cleansing the land under the direction of the Lord (which includes all of the elements listed above such as repentance and any necessary restitution) then we are ready to undertake the raising of the canopy over that area and pray the fear of the Lord as a declaration to the heavenlies and to the land (the community, the city).

Depending on the number of people involved in the initiative, we normally position groups at the cardinal, or exit and entry points surrounding each community or area being prayed over. At these points we pray specific and strategic implementation of the words and promises that the Lord will have given to us collectively. We are prophetically positioning the 'tent pegs' of the canopy of the Lord in this area.

We speak forth the severing of any shroud or any strongholds that need to be addressed, knowing that their 'fodder' and footholds have been removed through the earlier prayer strategies. There is never any room for any form of presumptuousness, since it is the Lord who is at work in and through His people. Together we jointly undertake the removal of whatever the Lord has shown that needs to be addressed. Bear in mind this is a prophetic act, which has been prayerfully and deliberately developed under the Lord's direction.

The area in question can be a church property, a business property, a community, an area of land in which a residential centre or ministry centre is located or even a city. Then at times our hands are raised before the Lord and we speak forth the raising of the canopy, often in song and in praise, and we give thanks to the Lord for what He has done, and will continue to do. Then we wait on the Lord to see if He wants to share anything else with us, since often this act of prophetic ministry brings further revelation and direction from the Lord, and we want to collate all that He has revealed to us.

It is a healthy and important exercise to take time to hand the entire initiative back to the Lord, freeing ourselves from any unnecessary sense of responsibility. At this point we begin the process of stewarding what He has entrusted to us, but on His terms!

SOME PRACTICAL STEPS

How do we put all this together? It is important to have a leadership team that is willing to work with each other, and understand each other's strengths and weaknesses. This is a team that prays together and seeks God's counsel together, one that minimizes secondary issues and maximizes primary issues. Such a team learns how to apply these principles of personal life initially, and then implement them corporately in their territory. Again, this template can be for a city, a business, a church, or a community.

On a practical basis, we have found that there are a number of steps, when taken prayerfully and as under the direction of the Lord, that can minimize ambiguity and backlash and maximize the advancing of the kingdom of God in their midst (Matthew 11:12). While not necessarily always in this order, we have found the following steps to be of significant help in determining God's blueprint plan for undertaking a prayer strategy which readily results in the fear of the Lord coming into that place.

> **Determine who else of like mind is in your area**. Undoubtedly, God will have called other people to this project as well. Simply ask the Lord to reveal who those people might be and that divine connections are made.

> **Determine regular times of meeting for prayer and relationship building**. This is non-negotiable and in most authentic models of transformation and revival in this day and age, there have always been a small group of people who were willing to pay that price in seeking the whole counsel of God and implementing whatever He showed them, starting with their own lives. This is not a casual

'band–aid process'. This is a partnership with God in which when the fear of the Lord is released, He will then confide in them (Psalm 25:14).

Determine who has done any similar research in the past. Invariably, over the years, God will have given different people various parts of the divine puzzle. It is a matter of praying those people into place. It can be surprising and thrilling to see who some of these people might be who are just waiting to be released by the Lord.

Come together often for times of envisioning and encouragement since, from this, a higher level of trust and cooperation develops. Proverbs 11:14 reminds us: *"For lack of guidance a nation falls, but many advisers make victory sure."* As people come together, God brings revelation and insight to His people. Proverbs 24:6 indicates that victory is won through many advisers and that guidance is needed to wage war. Such meetings become invaluable for on–going training as well as for the developing of greater trust and common vision among all the participants.

Determine who else (in isolation) may be part of God's developing strategy and who needs to be invited, brought out and encouraged. In other words, ask the Lord who is missing and who may need to be invited.

Collate any and all prophetic words and/or earlier attempts in developing a transformation template and determine what happened. Past failures very often will hold the key to unlocking the strategies that God now wants to implement. We have often found that when words, insights and promises from the Lord over a period of years are collated they thrill and inspire those who have now come together — recognizing that this has been on God's heart for many years. These very people have now become the present–day catalysts for change.

Ask leaders and intercessors to determine three main strengths and weakness of the area. This will invariably require homework and observation in order that people can focus in on the unique purposes for which God has called that place into being. We want to avoid any familiarity that has given place to complacency and lethargy.

Determining weaknesses often gives insight and understanding to what the mindsets and strongholds are that still influence an area. Again we can become so familiar with these hindrances or problems that they have become part of everyday life. When we ask the Lord to reveal to us what is out of order, then we can more readily see what has to be addressed. Often these issues reveal the opposite of God's primary redemptive purposes in that area.

Develop researchers and intercessors under leadership teams, ensuring that these people are correctly trained in a manner that builds up the entire body. Several training resources are available developed by many ministry organizations including ourselves at Partnership Ministries.

Determine what is involved in your assigned and attainable area. This is the combination of good solid research based upon prayer that knows how to combine the objective and the subjective carefully. We are implementing the gift sets of those who are involved in the initiative but minimizing the use of over–subjectivity. Along with this, however, is the importance of knowing your assigned territory.

In *God's Design for Challenging Times,*[4] we deliberately shared on key principles concerning our boundaries. Protocol and accountability are important to the Lord, and we need to know that *"the boundary lines have fallen for me in pleasant places; surely I have a delightful inheritance."* (Psalm 16:6)

Both physical and spiritual boundaries need to be understood in any prayer project. The seven sons of Sceva are a timely reminder for those who feel they can minister outside of their boundary lines (Acts 19:13–16). When boundaries of authority and one's ministry are fully understood, we minimize casualties and maximize gain for the kingdom of God. Consequently the reminder of 2 Corinthians 10:15–16 can be of great encouragement as long as we understand the protocol of God's timing: *"Neither do we go beyond our limits by boasting of work done by others. Our hope is that, as your faith continues to grow, our area of activity among you will greatly expand, so that we can preach the gospel in the regions beyond you…"*

Develop contact with those in surrounding areas. This enables us to keep a healthy perspective on what we are dealing with since, in many cases, our at–home issues are a reflection of situations beyond our boundaries. Being informed in this manner will often authenticate the manner and substance of our prayers. This also enables us to receive input from those in other areas who are praying for us, and who are not limited or affected by the spiritual issues and strongholds we might be dealing with in our home environment.

With the leadership group continuously seeking the direction and unction of the Lord, gradually see the 'jigsaw pieces' emerge and connect. This will involve the 'correct stewarding' of new ground and insights that the Lord entrusts to us. In our book *Transformed! People – Cities – Nations,*[5] we reviewed the ten principles for sustaining genuine revival. Over the years we have amassed a number of testimonies through hands–on research that determined why certain moves of God came to an end — either abruptly or over a period of time. These ten reasons, when reversed, can actually become ten keys for stewarding what God intends us to restore, which is what we term as the "guard, keep and occupy principle".

At all times we continue to heed the promises of Hebrews 7:25, Romans 8:26, Romans 8:34, Isaiah 53:12d, Hosea 6:1–3, Isaiah 62:6–7 in that it is God who is working in and through us in the power of the Holy Spirit. He is the one that is leading us, guiding us, directing us, informing us and urging us on since He is the one wanting to restore the fullness of His purposes for us. We need constantly to remind ourselves of the wonderful promise in Philippians 1:6 — *"…being confident of this, that He who began a good work in you will carry it on to completion until the day of Christ Jesus."*

Ensure that, whenever repentance is required as the Lord directs and reveals, it is undertaken with prayer and accountability since this is the power of the Cross at work in our midst. Then as already stated, we look to see if there is a place for restitution in order that whatever the kingdom of God requires, is done.

THE GUARD, KEEP AND OCCUPY PRINCIPLE

In our book *Transformed!*[6] we have referred to this "guard, keep and occupy principle" mentioned above which is evident in Scripture –

> *"When an evil spirit comes out of a man, it goes through arid places seeking rest and does not find it. Then it says, 'I will return to the house I left.' When it arrives, it finds the house swept clean and put in order. Then it goes and takes seven other spirits more wicked than itself, and they go in and live there. And the final condition of that man is worse than the first."* (Luke 11:24–26)

> The Matthew 12:44–45 parallel to this passage states: *"…When it arrives, it finds the house unoccupied, swept clean and put in order… the final condition of that man is worse than the first… That is how it will be with this wicked generation."*

This stewardship principle is referred to in *Transformed!*[7] Our work needs to be continually stewarded, since it is possible that vulnerabilities and oversights and changes within our areas of responsibility may cause breaches in our relationships and corporate times of prayer, thus lowering our guard. We may well think a project is done and finished, requiring no more time and attention. In fact, it is usually quite the contrary!

THE STORY OF ZOE — AND THE GREAT ESCAPE!

Our younger son and his family decided to adopt a dog on one occasion. It quickly became friends with our oldest grandson Elijah. No one is quite aware of the origin of Zoe but she does have her own perspective on life! Once, when our family was visiting us, the dog was being looked after by friends. During their journey, the call came that Zoe had escaped the safety of the yard through a hole in the fence. Our son and his wife were very concerned as to how they would share this news with Elijah and his younger brother. This was particularly concerning since cougars are known to roam in the area in which they live, and little puppies could be a rather enticing delicacy.

Just as they were about to leave us, word came that Zoe had been found. There was great excitement and relief for everyone. However as they were proceeding homewards, word came again that Zoe had once again escaped; in fact, through the same hole in the same fence! The weaknesses in the fence had not been addressed.

If we do not keep our 'spiritual firewalls' in place, and we do not correctly steward what God has entrusted to us, and we do not repair any breaches that occur in our areas of responsibility — whether personally or corporately — the enemy can once again penetrate. There is a happy ending in that once they had returned home, Elijah and his dad along with many others searched for Zoe and she was finally found. This time, the hole in the fence was repaired, but not before several important lessons had been learned.

KEEP WATCH!

Regular prayer walking and regular prayer vigilance is required especially as a business, church, community or city grows and develops. We want to ensure that, even as new stewardship issues continue to occur through people who may come to that area, our vigilance, care and responsibility for what God has entrusted to us also continues. This is one of the main reasons why revivals enter into attrition long before their God–appointed duration. They may begin to wane before God's transforming power affects the systems of life in that area, and even before the fear of the Lord is established in the life of the people.

It is a decision that we need to enter into for ourselves, and then make a choice to pray this into our communities with integrity and purity and understanding:

> *"He will be the sure foundation for your times, a rich store of salvation and wisdom and knowledge; the fear of the Lord is the key to this treasure."* (Isaiah 33:6)

We are God's prophetic voice for society. We have been called to sound the alarm for such a time such as this!

What amazing words! The fear of the Lord is the key to this treasure of salvation and wisdom and knowledge. What more can be said?

In the pages of this book I have sought to give as much insight as possible into the fear of the Lord and how this can be applied at both a personal and also a corporate level. In the end, however, it comes down to the individual and our own response to what God is saying to us on this matter.

Our visit to Darwin was impacting and sobering! Those crocodiles in Kakadu were active and watching for any opportunity to attack unsuspecting prey. We, the church, need to be vigilant and not allow the enemy to gain any ground or foothold, due to ignorance, complacency or apathy. We are God's prophetic voice for society. We have been called to sound the alarm for such a time such as this!

In the coming days there will be an increasing need for the people of God to understand and appropriate both these truths: that we live and work in the fear of God, but also within the love of God.

Both constitute the character of God. As the Psalmist puts it: *"Let those who fear the Lord say: 'His love endures forever.'"* (Psalm 118:4) He goes on to say: *"...the Lord delights in those who fear Him, who put their hope in His unfailing love."* (Psalm 147:11)

Until the return of the Lord, this will be our mandate: *"He said in a loud voice, 'Fear God and give Him glory, because the hour of His judgment has come. Worship Him who made the heavens, the earth, the sea and the springs of water.'"* (Revelation 14:7)

My prayer for each of us is that we will choose to allow the Lord to meet with us with such measure that, as we allow His fear to enter into every part of our being, we can never possibly be the same again, and that we become salt and light that will open up the eyes and hearts of our communities and cities in preparation for His return.

> *" The greatness of God rouses fear within us, but His goodness encourages us not to be afraid of Him. To fear and not be afraid — that is the paradox of faith."* A.W. Tozer [8]

ENDNOTES

Introduction:

1. *God's Design for Challenging Times* by Rev. Dr. Alistair Petrie – Published by CHI–Books PO Box 6462, Upper Mount Gravatt, QLD 4122 Australia ISBN 978–0–9870891–0–6

2. *God's Design for Challenging Times* by Rev. Dr. Alistair Petrie – Chapter 4 and 5 – Published by CHI–Books PO Box 6462, Upper Mount Gravatt, QLD 4122 Australia ISBN 978–0–9870891–0–6

Chapter 1:

1. *Analytical concordance to the Holy Bible* by Robert Young – Page 72 – United Society for Christian literature, Lutterworth Press, Gulliford and London – Reprint 1975. ISBN 0–7188–0021–4

2. *Analytical concordance to the Holy Bible* by Robert Young – Page 66 – United Society for Christian literature, Lutterworth Press, Gulliford and London – Reprint 1975. ISBN 0–7188–0021–4

3. *Analytical concordance to the Holy Bible* by Robert Young – regarding yir'ah, yare' – Page 55, 53 – United Society for Christian literature, Lutterworth Press, Gulliford and London – Reprint 1975. ISBN 0–7188–0021–4

4. *Analytical concordance to the Holy Bible* by Robert Young – Page 33 – United Society for Christian literature, Lutterworth Press, Gulliford and London – Reprint 1975. ISBN 0–7188–0021–4

5. A.W. Tozer quotes – www.goodreads.com

6. *New American Standard Version,* The Lockman Foundation; 1995 Printing as used on Bible Gateway www.biblegateway.com

7. *New English Translation Version,* The Lockman Foundation; 1995 Printing as used on Bible Gateway www.biblegateway.com

8. *Revised Standard Version,* London Oxford University Press; 1971

9. *Analytical concordance to the Holy Bible* by Robert Young – Page 85 – United Society for Christian literature, Lutterworth Press, Gulliford and London – Reprint 1975. ISBN 0–7188–0021–4

10. *Analytical concordance to the Holy Bible* by Robert Young – regarding yir'ah, yare' – Page 55, 53 – United Society for Christian literature, Lutterworth Press, Gulliford and London – Reprint 1975. ISBN 0–7188–0021–4

11. *Revised Standard Version,* London Oxford University Press; 1971

Chapter 2:

1. *Amplified Bible* (AMP), Published by The Lockman Foundation, 1987 Printing version as used on Bible Gateway www.biblegateway.com

2. *Common English Bible* (CEB), 2011 Bible Gateway www.biblegateway.com

3. *Good News Translation* (GNT), Canadian Bible Society (CBS), Toronto, ON, ISBN 0–88834–044–3

4. *The Message* (MSG), 2011 Bible Gateway www.biblegateway.com

5. *Intimate Friendship with God* by Joy Dawson, Chosen Books a Division of Baker Book House, Grand Rapids, MI 49516 – 1986 ISBN 0–8007–9084–7

6. *The Fear of the Lord* by John Bevere – Creation House, Orlando, Florida 1997 ISBN 0–88419–486–8

7. *The Fear of the Lord* by John Bevere – Page 75 – Creation House, Orlando, Florida 1997 ISBN 0–88419–486–8

8. Ibid. – Page 78

9. Ibid. – Page 80

10. *Intimate Friendship with God* by Joy Dawson – Page 39 – Chosen Books a Division of Baker Book House, Grand Rapids, MI 49516 – 1986 ISBN 0–8007–9084–7

11. Ibid. – Page 39

12. Ibid. – Page 41

13. Quote from Duncan Campbell as referred to by Dr. Michael Brown in a web article entitled *America Needs a Revival of the Fear of God* – www.christianpost.com.

Chapter 3:

1. *God's Design for Challenging Times* by Rev. Dr. Alistair Petrie – Published by Chi Books, PO Box 6462, Upper Mt Gravatt, QLD 4122, Australia – 2013 – ISBN 978–0–9870891–0–6

2. A.W. Tozer quotes – www.worldofquotes.com

3. *God's Design for Challenging Times* by Rev. Dr. Alistair Petrie – Published by Chi Books, PO Box 6462,Upper Mt Gravatt, QLD 4122, Australia – 2013 – ISBN 978–0–9870891–0–6

4. Quote from Duncan Campbell as referred to by Dr. Michael Brown in a web article entitled *America Needs a Revival of the Fear of God* – www.christianpost.com.

5. Loren Cunningham – *A Conversation on a Leaders Heart* – www.fathersofthefaith.com

Chapter 4:

1. Duncan Campbell, *The Lewis Awakening*, 1949–1953 – Page 14–1

2. Duncan Campbell, *The Lewis Awakening* – www.shilohouse.org

3. Ibid.

4. Some of these facts and details have been based on several personal visits to the Hebrides as well as interviewing many people who had firsthand experience – some who are now with the Lord.

Chapter 5:

1. *Whatever Happened to Worship* by A.W. Tozer – Page 30–31 – Published by WingSpread Publishers, 1985

2. *The Fear of the Lord* by John Bevere – Chapter 14, Pages 187 to 193 – Creation House, Orlando, Florida 1997 ISBN 0–88419–486–8

3. The Sentinel Group – *An Appalachian Dawn* – www.sentinelgroup.org

4. *Amplified Bible* (AMP), Published by The Lockman Foundation, 1987 Printing version as used on Bible Gateway www.biblegateway.com

5. *Transformations* DVD – The Sentinel Group — www. sentinelgroup.org

6. Ibid.

Chapter 6:

1. *God's Design for Challenging Times* by Rev. Dr. Alistair Petrie – Page 107–110 – Published by CHI–Books PO Box 6462, Upper Mount Gravatt, QLD 4122 Australia ISBN 978–0–9870891–0–6

2. *Releasing Heaven on Earth* by Rev Dr. Alistair Petrie – by Sovereign World Ltd. – ISBN 978–1852404819. Available through Partnership Ministries – www.partnershipministries.org

3. Ibid. Page 85

4. *God's Design for Challenging Times* by Rev. Dr. Alistair Petrie – Published by CHI–Books PO Box 6462, Upper Mount Gravatt, QLD 4122 Australia ISBN 978–0–9870891–0–6

5. *Transformed–People–Cities–Nations* by Rev Dr. Alistair Petrie Published by Sovereign World Ltd. – ISBN 978–1–85240–482–6. Available through Partnership Ministries – www.partnershipministries.org

6. Ibid.

7. Ibid.

8. *The Knowledge of the Holy* by A.W. Tozer

About The Author

Rev. Dr Alistair P. Petrie

For many years in both the United Kingdom and Canada, Alistair served as senior pastor in diverse city church settings. With that experience and his earlier years spent in professional broadcasting, he now serves as the Executive Director of Partnership Ministries, a global ministry that teaches the principles and relevance of the Gospel and its relationship to the wider Church, the Marketplace, to Cities and to Nations. Partnership Ministries is positioned as a ministry for the 21st Century Church and combines prayer and research to prepare for lasting revival, authentic transformation and the release of Kingdom culture. In doing so, Alistair consults regularly with churches and ministries, businesses, and business leaders helping them in applying the principles of Transformation in their areas of influence — and explains how this releases cities and nations into their respective destinies.

Alistair travels extensively to many nations researching and teaching these transformation principles, in both church and city settings as well as in the marketplace arena. Obtaining his Doctorate through Fuller Seminary, he has been a guest lecturer at several academic settings and Schools of Ministry. As well as being an international speaker, he is the author of several books, and along with his ministry team has produced an informative DVD teaching series. He is married to Marie and along with their two sons, Mike and Richard, their entire family serve the wider church and the Marketplace in the global arena.

Partnership Ministries
www.partnershipministries.org